Writer's Publishing Workbook

The Absolute Indie Workbook Series
(Contains full text of original book)

Jo Robinson

ISBN-13: 978-1533636720
ISBN-10: 1533636729

DEDICATION

To You – Fabulous Writer

CONTENTS

ABOUT THIS BOOK

This is the workbook version of The Absolute Indie, containing both the full text of the original book as well as the interactive section for your own writing and publishing information. In this book I'm going to share with you the things you need to know to self-publish your book on Amazon and CreateSpace, as well as a few tips and tricks that I've learned on my own journey to being the Absolute Indie. In addition to all you'll be needing along your publishing journey, in this workbook you'll find pages to take notes and keep records of all the information relevant to your particular book/s, thereby ensuring that you never need to spend any time at all in the future hunting for things written down months or years ago, the locations of which forgotten or misplaced.

I'll be using Windows 7 for screenshots here, as I have yet to try using the apparently fabulous Mac. Feel free to email me if you need further help at theabsoluteindie@gmail.com. I'll also be using another two easy to operate programmes, which are free to download, and I'll be showing you exactly where to find them, so there's no need for you to worry about having to pay for any fancy new software, or to learn any mind-boggling techno-jargon. My aim is not to overwhelm, but to help, by keeping the whole process as simple as possible. This book is especially for the author who is publishing for the first time, but also for already published Indies who have little or no budget to outsource all of the formatting and design parts of getting their books to readers.

While being a book showing you how to proceed from writing the first page of your book to publishing it and beyond, I wanted to create an interactive experience for you, the writer. On my own Indie journey I often found it exasperating having to dig for my various pieces of instructional material for all the things that need to be done along the way. With this workbook, everything you need is in one place, including everything you need for your very own book, for easy reference at every step. And for those days when the words won't come, and that old blank screen refuses to go away, head on over to the Procrastination Palace section for a little bit of silliness or inspiration to get you going again.

I've tried to keep all instructions as plain and straightforward as possible, but as I said before, if there is anything here that you find confusing, please send me an email and I promise to answer you. As long as I'm alive that is. If you're reading a very old and tattered version of this book, then it could very well be that I have expired, in which case I apologise. For now, let the adventure begin.

WHAT IS THE ABSOLUTE INDIE?

Absolute Indies are those of us who not only write books, but also have complete control of our own publishing businesses. The Absolute Indie doesn't necessarily go it alone, and has the choice of outsourcing various jobs needed along the way, such as purchasing professionally designed book covers and paying for editing or proofreading services, but also has the knowledge of how to do these things should the need or desire arise. Absolute Indies are self-employed. As well as writing the books that they love, they manage their time and their business as the CEO of their company, with the end aim being to publish what they write as perfectly as they can.

Why this book? Because this is the book I would have liked to have had when I considered publishing my own first novel. I started my trip as an Absolute Indie from a very deeply damaged Zimbabwe, where PayPal is not available and getting a credit card meant getting one from another country, so I had no access to paid help. It took a lot of work, research, and yes, some blood, sweat and tears – alright then, maybe not actual blood – but it was quite an epic journey from total cluelessness. I've discovered that there's always more to learn as I grow as an Indie, and I'm always happy to find out some new thing from those magical author heroes who have already been there, and now lead the way. One of the most wonderful things in the community of authors all over the world is their willingness to share what they learn with others at various stages in the craft. We aren't competitors. We're comrades, all of us Indies, now changing the face of publishing forever. This book is because I want to share what I've learned so far with those new to independent publishing, in the hopes of making their journeys towards getting their books to readers as painless as it can be even when they don't have much money available.

You don't have to do it all yourself, and if you can afford to pay for needed services, you really should. Our aim is not for typo-ridden books or bad cover art. If you can't afford to though, then you can do it all yourself, and with a little extra dedication, your creative soul can turn to the technical things if publishing quality books is what it desires. Amazon has opened up the world of being published authors for all of us, and you really do see books of all kinds there. The strange and the weird. The out of print and the just plain out there. The world of publishing is the Indie writer's oyster now, and we should try and make sure that our end product has a great appearance in addition to being a fabulous read. I have often seen comments made by some very successful authors emphatically stating that if you don't pay for professional cover design and editing, you're better off not self-publishing your work, and thereby sullying the reputation of all. I strongly disagree if a writer believes in their work, but simply can't afford to pay for professional services. What a shame not to be able to share your wonderful stories with readers because of a cash flow problem. Rather, take on the challenge of going the extra mile to produce the best book you can. Go slow and steady, and make the biggest effort that you can. Research and learn. Learn all that you have to learn, and don't allow the lack of cash to pay for these things stop you from achieving your dream.

Whether you've unsuccessfully submitted your book to traditional publishers, or made the decision to self-publish to retain control of your work without having tried that route, and have absolutely no clue how to go about it, the object of The Absolute Indie is to help you do just that. The world of independent publishing has gained much credence these past few years. We have some mighty scribblers in our club now, who are making loads of cash. No longer are Indie authors seen as traditionally published wannabes, but with this emerging credibility comes the fact that self-published books must be able to run with the big boys as far as the finished product is concerned. Your aim must be to produce a book of the same quality and standard as any traditionally published book, or better, and yes, that is possible.

I never set out to do everything myself on my publishing journey and not spend a cent. It wasn't because I was a tightwad. As I said, I was living in a country at the time where the banking system had collapsed and PayPal was sanctioned. Back then it seemed like the only way to pay for proofing services or a professional cover design was through PayPal. I was stumped. I didn't have much of an online presence then, and the couple of people I did ask for help either wanted me to take them on as my publisher and give them a portion of my royalties, or find another way to pay them. I couldn't find another way to pay them, and I didn't want to sign with a small publisher. I wanted all my royalties, and I wanted final control of what went into and on my book. Stubborn scribbler that I was, I jumped in boots and all, and learned how to become an Absolute Indie along the way. Again, I stress that I don't recommend that you don't pay for proofreading or professional cover design if you can afford it. The quality of both of these things can make or break a book. Trust me. I learned the hard way. The Absolute Indie doesn't just know how to publish a book. They know that quality must be their cornerstone, and they make it their business to know their business.

I made lots of mistakes along the way, but that's good for you now, because I get to show you how not to fall into the same holes that I did. I can honestly say that I haven't read many eBooks where I never picked up a single typo, and I'm including traditionally published eBooks here. That's not to say that I'm condoning typos and grammar gremlins. Big name authors can get away with these things. Indies can't. With the rise of self-publishing, and so many jumping on to the bandwagon, some appallingly bad works have been published. Unsuspecting readers downloaded books riddled with errors or just plain badly written and put together, and then vowed never to buy an Indie book again. This still happens, and it really is not what we want, so we must work harder to make sure that we stand out from the crowd in a good way. Our aim is to produce our books as close to perfection as we can get them, and having other eyeballs proofread your book is a very big deal before you publish. There are ways to do this without breaking the bank if you really don't have any spare cash at all, but a burning need to share your awesome story with the world, so not to worry. Knowing your limitations is the best place to begin to work your way around them, without having to sell all your granny's antique teapots to finance your book.

I had an ancient dinosaur of a computer when I wrote my first book, and very tenuous connection to the internet. I was also about as computer and IT savvy as garden fungus. Looking back now I shudder at my clueless bravado. One really great decision I made back then was to write and publish a short story by way of practice. Short stories weren't something I had written before, even though I've loved to read them all my life. There's an art to writing a good short, and I didn't think that I had it. Still, it had to be done, so I did it. If you are totally new to self-publishing, I suggest you do too. This will teach you the nuts and bolts of the publication process and get you started on your actual Indie journey in a less terrifying way than if you zoom out the gates with your life's work. Make sure that it's the best short story that you can write though. Short stories are very popular on Amazon. I personally buy loads of them, and have authors I love who only ever write short. Life is busy in this world of ours and a short story can be just as satisfying as a novel when schedules are crazy but we still want a read. You don't have to do this of course. You can go right ahead and launch your big boy first. It's true though that sometimes we don't know how awesome something will be until we try it. Terror or not, once I'd got my first words down, my little tale flew, and I discovered a new love of writing shorts.

In the spirit of The Absolute Indie, I have purposely created this book entirely without any outside help at all – including the services of so much as a single proofreader other than myself, and using only free resources. In my current Absolute Indie world I do pay for proofreading and other services, such as you definitely should if you can afford it, but I want to show you that you can do the whole thing on your own, with a budget of 0.00, so I'm holding thumbs that there aren't any typos lurking here. Once again, in the spirit of The Absolute Indie, if you do find a typo in this book, or any other thing that offends your sensibilities, I'd be very grateful to hear about it from you at theabsoluteindie@gmail.com.

WHAT CAN YOU PUBLISH ON AMAZON

Have a look at Amazon's guidelines to make sure that your content meets their criteria. Obviously the words that you publish must be your own. You must be the copyright holder of everything between the covers of your book, unless it is legal to use. You pretty much have free rein other than what you see listed by them as not acceptable. You can publish anything from How to Make Toe Socks to the steamiest erotica, and everything in between. You can publish short stories and essays. Books for children. You can even publish your family tree if that's what you fancy. Probably only your family will buy it, but that's your choice, and you'll have something to pass down to future generations. Follow your passion.

You don't have to stick to publishing one genre. Neither do you have to choose only either fiction or non-fiction. As The Absolute Indie only you decide what you will publish. Make up your own brand new genre if you want to. Do you have a hobby or an ability that you are knowledgeable about? An ailment you know intimately, or something that you have overcome? Are you a kitchen king or queen with a stack of wonderful recipes that you'd love to share? You can write about all of these things too. Self help books are very popular. If you like writing naughty stories, or about a topic that you don't want people you know to connect you to, you have the choice of using a pen name rather than your real one.

Copyright and Fair Use

When it comes to copyright infringement for both content and images, it is always better to err on the side of caution. Unless you're a hundred percent certain that using someone else's work can't possibly get you sued, don't use it. When it comes to this issue, ignorance of the law doesn't count. You are always at fault even if you don't know what copyright means, so as the leader of your Indie realm, you must set about finding out, before blissfully nabbing some gorgeous creation floating around on the internet and plonking it in or on your own work, and then possibly finding yourself in a whole world of trouble.

When I was new to blogging, and still in my clueless world of smiley unicorns where copyright for online images wasn't in my frame of reference, I zoomed around the internet looking for pictures for my posts. Whenever I found one from random Google searches I downloaded them and added them at will. I quiver with relief at my own past IT ineptitude that led me to accidentally and permanently delete my entire photo gallery from my blog site in one fell swoop. Now I have old blog posts with no images at all, and not a lot of time on my hands to replace them, but at least I know that there isn't some copyrighted image lurking in there that could cost me big, not because I'm a conscious thief, but because I didn't take the time to find out if what I was doing was legal. There are some truly great free images out there if you know where to look though, and I'll be showing those places to you when we get around to creating a book cover.

While titles of books are not subject to copyright, and you can use them as you please, the content of books and also songs are very much so, unless they are clearly in the public domain. Stay well away from music. Never use song lyrics in your books without specific written permission from the copyright holders, unless you are positive that they are in the public domain – not even a single recognisable sentence. It's not worth the risk. Legally, using a phrase of ten words or less is considered fair use if you're happy to take the chance. Plain lists can't be copyrighted. For instance, a list of varieties of birds. Recipes can't be copyrighted either. Unless you actually do copy and paste another writer's recipes exactly that is.

WHY SHOULD YOU PUBLISH ON AMAZON

The first and most obvious reason is that Amazon is the biggest retailer of eBooks in the world, with millions of customers already there and buying those books. I only buy eBooks from Amazon, and so do many people. Your self-published book will be up there rubbing shoulders with the books of bestselling authors, and if you go about producing quality eBooks and paperbacks, most readers won't realise that you are an Indie author, so your chances of success are as good as any if your stories are enjoyed.

I wrote my first book with a pen in a pile of notebooks before I was connected to the internet at all. The only reason that I did connect to the internet was because I thought that I needed to find an agent. I set up a Facebook account and looked for writer's groups to connect to, and was, I'm ashamed to say, a little suspicious when I first came across Indie authors, firm in my belief back then that unless you'd cleared the gatekeepers and were traditionally published you were a fake author. Pretty soon I realised that not only were many Indies earning their living with their books, some of them had hit NYT bestseller status all completely under their own steam.
It wasn't long before I became an avid Indie. It's a longer journey, and needs hard work and patience, but the reward is there to be had. It turns out that there are gatekeepers for self-published authors after all. Readers. If readers love your books, you will eventually gain more. A traditionally published book has a huge advantage out of the gates, and while the road to success for the Indie author involves a lot of hard work and patience, if done to the best of our ability, self-publishing is just as legitimate as traditionally published at the end of the day, because your books will fly or fall as your readership grows purely on their own merit.

You have total control of the content and cover of your book when you self-publish. Traditional publishers have editors. Editors don't always see things the way that you do, and you have to make the changes that they request. You can disagree with them, but they have the final say.
As an Indie, you choose your cover design according to your own vision. Traditional publishers get to choose your book cover. You have no say in the matter.

Traditional publishers take their time. It takes months and months before your book will see the light of day. The Absolute Indie publishes the book when the book is ready. No waiting.
Indies keep all of our royalties, which might not work out to a massive pile in the beginning, but a few years down the line when you have an established readership and backlist, you could very well give up any day job you might still be doing.

Obviously, if you get an offer from a traditional publisher with a big fat advance and the knowledge that your book will be sold in bookstores, you can grab it as fast as you like, but if your book is with a small press selling few copies, you'll just get a smaller cut of an already small pie. If that's what you really want though, then don't stop submitting your books the traditional way. The beauty of self-publishing means that you can submit traditionally and publish Indie at the same time. You can sell your already self-published book at any time because you own it. What we are seeing a lot of these days is already traditionally published authors now starting to self-publish new works. The publishing world is completely different to what it was a few years ago, and self-publishing is very much a part of the fabric of it, so wear your Indie badge with pride.

Small Presses

I like to know about all my possible future options, even thought at this point I'm not considering anything other than self-publishing, so I found out what's available to us. I have several author friends who are very happy with their small press publishers. There are really good ones but there are also some very bad ones. To be clear here, anyone can set themselves up as a publisher if they know how to publish books on the very same sites that we Indies publish on. You hand over your manuscript and they would then (hopefully) edit it, format it, supply a cover for it, and publish it. They should also offer marketing for it. They have total control of the book and send you whatever agreed portion of royalties you are due to you when they get them. They decide how much to charge for your book, and if you feel that the price is too high to sell, there's nothing you can do about that. You don't know how many books are sold this way until they let you know, whereas you have complete knowledge when you self-publish. Having said that, there are authors who really don't want to have to deal with anything other than writing, and for them the small press is often a joyful find, and they work very well together.

If that becomes the case for you, then try and find a press that is recommended, and do your homework first. Google them, and read all that you can find about them. Speak to other authors who have signed this way first, and be very cautious before you sign anything. There are many, many horror stories out there of badly edited books being published by some small presses, with the author having absolutely no power to fix them. Royalties not being paid properly or not at all is another thing, and at the end of the day when it comes to marketing, unless you're a big name author you're going to have to do most of it yourself anyway. If as a new author you're only selling a few books to begin with, why give part of your earnings away when you don't have to? Consider that if you do sign a contract with any small press, it's going to be a huge nightmare if you find that you want or need to get out of it.

The Absolute Indie has total control of their income and expenditure, and always has the power to change anything in or on their books any time they choose to, not to mention using pricing promotions as they choose to in their marketing efforts.

Vanity Publishers

In a nutshell, a vanity publisher simply charges you to publish your book. But, and this is a big but, some of them bind you with contracts in addition to that, always wanting more and more cash from you. Don't go anywhere near those guys. Either your publisher pays you according to your agreed contract, or you can pay to have your books published without a contract. You have to purchase your own books from a couple of these publishers, and then sell them yourself even though they hold the rights to your book. This should never be an option. There are honest publishers out there who will charge you to publish your book, and that's fine if you prefer not to deal with the process, but don't sign any contract giving them the rights to your book as well. You can still pay for services as an Indie if you really don't want to do certain things in the publishing process yourself while retaining all the rights to your book. Don't ever sign anything without having someone who really knows about these things go over it for you. Better still, learn your business from top to bottom and do it for yourself.

Hugh Howey and many other self-published authors have proved that Indies can achieve substantial respect, and bucket loads of cash also. In an interview I once read, Hugh attributed his success to hard work, patience, and a little bit of luck. You could get lucky. In fact I really hope that you do. Having your book fall into the right hands at the right time could rocket you to stardom. It might happen. But only if it's out there waiting to fall into those hands. You have just as much chance at success as a self-published author as anyone else if you do the work, and if you change your mind at any point, you're safe in the knowledge that you can pitch a self-published book to a traditional publisher at any future time that you fancy, because you hold all the rights to it. Just like Hugh Howey you can do both, and be a hybrid publisher with some of your books traditionally published and others published the Indie way.

WRITING YOUR BOOK

Even though this book is intended to show you the nuts and bolts of how to publish your first book on Amazon, what scribbler can avoid the opportunity to share a few thoughts on the actual writing of books? Not this one. Those seasoned people of the pen who are only here for the tools, feel free to bounce ahead to the bits you're after. This is for the newbies here, a few tiny things I wish I knew when I first began my writing journey. I will say one nut and bolt thing firstly though.

Ideally, you should find out the basics of how to self-publish your book before you start writing it. Trying to format a book full of glitches that you only find out are glitches when the time comes to load your completed manuscript can be a nightmare. Manuscript formatting for CreateSpace and Amazon Kindle are completely different. I suggest writing your book on a clean unformatted document, without using tabs or spaces to indent, and then making copies when you're finished to format individually for each platform. If it's too late for that not to worry, we'll get to the how to soon enough. Also, you should create your publishing accounts on Amazon and CreateSpace as soon as you decide to self-publish, even if you haven't started to write your first book yet, and familiarise yourself with them and make sure they're ready to rock when you're ready to rock. You're going to be nervous enough when the time comes without the need for the stresses of filling in forms.

As far as how to write your book is concerned, obviously that is entirely up to you. There are many books out there on the actual process of writing that you could buy. My personal favourite is Stephen King's On Writing. If you feel a little shaky concerning grammar and punctuation, then buy William Strunk's Manual of Style. In fact even if you're not wobbly in this regard, buy it anyway. All writers should have these two books in my humble opinion. I do believe that we learn to write by reading, and that no writing course or book can impart the magic needed to weave a tale, but getting the grammar wrong can really spoil a book, no matter how beautiful the story is. Our brains pick up much more than just a story when we read a book. I believe that the knowledge of how to write is imparted in the reading of the writings of others.

The most important thing I have to share about learning how to write is that you probably already know how to write, and you'll figure that out quickly when you just start doing it. The hardest thing for me to do was to write the first paragraph of my first novel, because I strongly believed that because I'd never attended a class on writing, or indeed been given any sort of information about what writers did to earn the golden ticket to being officially allowed to write for the consumption of actual readers, that I couldn't possibly get it right. Eventually that story clamoured so loudly in my head that I finally gave in and wrote the first page, thinking that seeing as how I hadn't mentioned this passion of mine to anyone, I could just throw it away, and nobody would ever know about my secret embarrassing attempt. I loved it though, and I wrote another page, and then another, and pretty soon there was no way that I could stop. The biggest mistakes I made with that book was over thinking every sentence, and over editing every single day. If you have the urge to write, just do it, and when you're done decide whether it's something you can do or not. You'll know.

There are prolific writers, and there are writers who produce only one book every year or two. This is again a very personal choice. It depends on what you want from your writing career. If you want to earn a living you're going to have to try and do more though, unless you have a breakout debut, your first book is not likely to make piles of money. J K Rowling can write a book a year and still make millions, but the new Indie won't as they zoom out through the starting gates.

The prolific writers will tell you that you must write every single day. Use it or lose it they say. Some go so far as to say that you should write not less than two or three thousand words per day. I agree that it's true that you should write every day if you can, even when you don't want to, with one tiny difference. I can honestly say that there's never been a time when I didn't want to write. There have been lots of times when I didn't want to write a particular thing though. For the one NaNoWriMo writing challenge I entered I did write a couple of thousand words every single day on just one book, and romped over the finish line ecstatic, laughing hysterically, and possibly with a family of itinerant rare pink candy beetles nesting in my hair, but do that every day for the rest of my life? No. I don't believe that the concept of writing every day should mean that you have to force yourself to staunchly write only your current book at a fixed rate of words per day until it's done before you can allow yourself to write anything else. If you enjoy that sort of thing then fine, but it sounds like torture to me.

If you don't write anything at all for a long time you will probably be a little rusty getting the old writing muscle back into condition, but you won't have lost your talent or ability. That lovely stuff will be with you always. I write several thousand words most days, barring illness or emergency, but not always on the same project, unless that's what I want to do. It's taken a couple of years from back when writing two thousand words a day left me tired and limp like an old rag, unable to contemplate anything harder to do than sitting down with a nice glass of wine. Now I know too - it is true, the more you write every day, the more you can write every day.

So if you really don't want to add writing to your book on any given day, then write something else for that day and return to your manuscript the next day. I wouldn't leave it for too long though. If you have a strong aversion to writing your book for any length of time then you should probably sit down and not get up again until you know exactly why that is. Is there a plot hole lurking in there and bothering you? Could there be a character getting up your nostril? Or could it be a much bigger problem in that you don't love what you're writing at all? Leaving a work in progress lying dormant for too long could mean that you'll never finish that book. When you get to a big roadblock like this then you really might have to force yourself to write through something you don't want to. To clear yourself from this scary place, just have at your keyboard, and carry on writing whether you think it's awful or not until you get out the other side. You will. The NaNoWriMo having to write the same book every day taught me that. That was my rule by the way, not NaNoWriMo's. Just push right on till the dam breaks. Your own mind is probably your biggest obstacle. If you really can't think of the next sentence, write around it. Move on to a scene beyond the one that has you stuck and come back to fix it later.

Are these stuck days writer's block? I have no idea. I think that writer's block is just plain old fear. Fear is an insidious thing that blocks us in so many aspects of our lives, and most of the time we don't even realise it. Writing a book and putting it naked and brand new out in to the world for all to see is a very big deal. Not a very great proportion of the people on the planet will even try, and of those who do try, the vast majority will give up before finishing. Those who push through don't find it smooth sailing from beginning to end. Lurking in the cobwebby recesses of your mind is always the fear, often disguised as something else. It's human nature for our minds to protect us from pains we've previously experienced. If you burn your hand on a stove, your mind will use fear to stop you from putting your hand on to a hot stove again so you don't have to experience that pain again. For emotional pain the fear is not as obvious.

We've all failed at something in life at some point. We've tried something and got it wrong. Maybe our friends on the playground had a good laugh at us, or maybe worse. We fear shame and the ridicule or the disdain of others. Your mind doesn't differentiate between the pain you felt when you failed to do a handstand and your buddies made you feel like a royal tool with their laughter, or the pain you might feel if your book is a failure and slaughtered in reviews, so it tries to stop you from finishing the book. It tries really hard to send you to the kitchen for a snack, or to the television, or to play Candy Crush instead. No pain there. Don't worry what the outcome will be for your book. Force your overprotective psyche to take a hike with full knowledge that this is not a fear to cave in to. Write through the fear even if you think that what you're writing is worse than turnip and marshmallow stew, because you'll probably find that when it's all finished and done you'll love what you've done. There'll be more than enough time to worry about what people think about it when it's published, so for now, just write it. Write it just for you.

That's another thing that can stop you in your tracks. Anytime that you're really not writing your book just for you. If you're trying to write a book because its genre is currently on trend, or you feel that it's something you should write to earn money, even though it's not something you love to read, you're unlikely to produce a great book. You maybe could force yourself through to the end, but it's very probable that you'll give up on it after a long slog. Giving it up is exactly what you should do as soon as possible if you really hate writing what you're producing. Close it up to ponder later, and start writing what you do love instead.

Any writer who can say with a straight face and truthful demeanour, that they have written not less than five hundred words and usually two thousand words every single day for the past twelve months is a very fortunate writer indeed. I have gone weeks without writing a single word purely because with this little thing we call life, stuff happens. People deal with divorce, cheating spouses, losses of day jobs, bereavements. All of that stuff happens to writers too. Sometimes these things can actually get us writing more, but mostly they just take time to deal with. Time away from writing. That's alright, because living is important, and if you haven't lived, you wouldn't have much to write about anyway. I've had some crazy things happen to me, but whenever I find my way back to my keyboard, the writing comes right back.

Plotters and Pantsers

To outline or not to outline. I do both. Each writer is as individual as a snowflake, and with time, form their own quirks and habits. Brand new writers as I was are generally clueless as to what works for them and what doesn't until they have a couple of books written. I started out as a major plotter. I plotted so much and for so long that writing my first novel was something that was less than writing a book than an outline which fortunately morphed into a story. I'd never spoken to another living writer at that point, or taken any form of course, so the joy of actually putting the story in my head to paper was slightly marred by the terror of not getting it perfectly right. Authors were magical creatures in ivory towers to me back then. They must have been taught how to write, and their talent must have shown itself straight away. I felt like an interloper for the longest time – a pretend writer – a wannabe fake. I only learned later that writers aren't taught as much as they're born. There's no specific formula. Whatever way suits you best is the right way for you.

Thank goodness I learned to pants a story too though. Much as I love reading sci-fi/fantasy, I truly believed that I couldn't write it. A couple of years ago when I saw the hype that is the NaNoWriMo I thought, why not? One month isn't much in a lifetime, and I thought it would be a hugely fun exercise to try and get the old writing muscle built up a little, not for one minute expecting to enjoy it. Enjoy it I did though, and at the end of it I had a finished novel, and a series planned. I didn't plan or plot. Every day I sat down at my computer without a clue as to what would happen next, believing strongly that this book would be a throwaway. My little pantsing experiment taught me that there doesn't have to be only one way to do things. I doubt that I'll ever do the NaNoWriMo again, but if you're starting out it can be a truly eye-opening experience, and the social part of it is great fun.

A Free Tool to Help You

Many authors love Scrivener, and it's easy to see why. It's not all that difficult to learn to navigate once you get stuck in, and the corkboard feature, as well as the ability to work with two different documents side by side at the same time is incredibly useful. It also makes getting your book ready to publish on Amazon really easy. If I had found it in the beginning of my Indie journey I would definitely have used it, but I've only recently explored it, and changing all of my habits now doesn't suit me. As for the purposes of this particular book, it is not always something that new Indies can afford to pay for, so I'll share a useful free tool available for you to use.
Firstly, you can view two different documents in Microsoft Word side by side too. Simply open both documents, and then click on View in the top ribbon, and select View Side by Side. When you want to go back to your single document, simply close the one you no longer need. This is especially useful when writing non-fiction and having to reference notes.

The second incredibly useful writer's helper comes in the form of free to download software called AllMyNotes even though it isn't only for writers. I create a folder for each new project, and then create notes within these for all the reference material I need. A different note for characters, scenes, locations and so on can be created, and it gives you a lovely corkboard effect when the folder is open. It also has the ability to link to any document on your computer or online, which is a lot better than wasting time searching through piles of files. It has all sorts of other features to help keep you organised, so download it and set it up to suit you.

Really Losing It

Unless you're writing your book the old fashioned way with pen and paper or printing it out as you go, you always stand the chance of losing it forever, unless you protect it rather than trusting your computer to do that for you. You're a writer, and not a techno wizard. I get it, but it would be wise to muzzle the technophobe within as best you can, and lock and load a couple of invisible fire breathing dragons. Your computer is the most valuable piece of equipment in your Indie publishing business, holding all your work, and you must do the best that you can to protect it from external harm. The ideal scenario is for you to purchase the best anti-virus, anti-malware, and general anti-hack attack software that you can afford. If you can't afford to pay for full packages, many excellent basic systems can be downloaded for free. These generally require you to regularly manually scan for invaders, but are worth this small effort if it means that your precious scribbles are protected from harm or malicious destruction. A couple to consider are Malware Bytes and Bitdefender.

Back up your computer regularly also. In the beginning of my writing journey, and as a clueless Luddite, I lost hundreds of thousands of words forever when my first computer crashed. I knew nothing about the damage that malware could do, and I had no backups of my work anywhere. I learned my lesson and now make sure that I make external copies of all my work on a daily basis. There are lots of places to choose from. You can pay for cloud storage or buy external storage devices. If money is tight you can simply email your work to yourself every day and store it in a back up folder for download just in case anything horrible happens to your computer. I still do this every day as well as saving my work onto my old laptop from my desktop regularly.

EDITING AND PROOFREADING

If the following steps seem like overkill, believe me, not even these are enough. I learned the hard way that trusting only yourself proofreading your work is a very slippery slope. The thought of publishing sloppy work was the last thing on my mind when I self-published my first book. I think that I'm pretty good at proofreading in general, so back then in my green days I was very confident that my book would be immaculate. I couldn't have been more wrong. Apart from the newbie error of not getting the page numbering to start in the right place in the paper version of the book, I made the further mistake of clicking an innocuous looking little button on CreateSpace which converted and loaded the print version on to Amazon for sale as an eBook. For quite a while it lurked there unbeknownst to me right beneath the correctly formatted eBook that I'd loaded. Readers bought not only the correct one, but that horribly corrupted book as well. There were words all over the place and massive white spaces. This was bad enough, but what made it much, much worse was that there were also typos that I'd not seen. The typos coupled with the awful formatting made for really bad reading experiences and three star reviews. I was pretty lucky that I didn't get completely buried in awful reviews, but the couple of low stars I did get that mentioned them were absolutely mortifying. The problem with bad reviews is they stay there even after you fix your mistakes, and short of un-publishing your book there isn't anything you can do about them. I still glow red just remembering that early blunder.

No matter how brilliant a writer you are, and no matter how immaculate your spelling and grammar generally are, the typos and glitches will still get in there. When you read your own writing, your brain knows what's supposed to be there and very often you'll see what you know should be there instead of the error that actually is. This quirk of the subconscious can also affect the way you read writing other than your own unless you're specifically looking for typos, so even with your extra eyeballs, they're most likely to still slip through. As I've said, there have been very few books I've read without so much as a single typo or grammar gremlin in both traditionally and self-published books. This doesn't mean that I'm saying that they're alright to leave in there. Take them out the minute you spot them. What I'm saying is that they are difficult little nasties to completely get rid of. Now that I do have easy access to proofreaders I definitely use them, but if you really can't afford to pay for this fairly pricy service, there are a few things that you can do to make up for the lack.

Book loving friends and family are a great help if they're prepared to help you look for problems in your book, but proofreading is a pretty specific skill, so you'd be much better off asking a fellow writer to swop this service with you, by proofing each other's work without having to pay. People who read a lot and people and are also writers are your best bets. If you can't find anyone willing to help you, you're going to have to put quite some time into this part of your Indie trip. There are a couple of tried and tested tricks to help you on your way though, so all is not lost.

Generally, after your own final draft edit, you would send your manuscript to your editor if you use one. There's no point in paying for proofreading twice, and the actual editing process will most probably mean more typos and gremlins to find. If you're not using an editor, then onward we go from your own final draft edit.

Step Away from the Book

After a final, thorough, and slow going through your normal spell checker, and the use of the Find function at the far right top of your screen to look for words that you know that you tend overuse or misspell, let your manuscript lie a while without so much as looking in its general direction. A week works for me, but longer is good. This is a good idea from a couple of perspectives. The effect of seeing the words you know should be there is going to be much stronger the closer you are to having written them. Also, apart from typos and grammatical errors, reading your manuscript with fresh eyes is a great help with finding plot bunnies or gaping holes. Take a week off. Read a book, or start on a new project, but don't even think about your manuscript or the story in it.

What a Fine Tale!

Make use of text to speech software such as Google's free SpeakIt app, or any other text to speech tools that you have access to. That computerised voice speaking your typos is very effective. Next, print it out on paper, and head off somewhere comfy. Somewhere that you don't usually write. Pour yourself a relaxing drink and start reading. Read it out loud as well. I know this sounds a little strange, but it really works. Hearing your own voice might incite a chuckle or two, adding to your relaxation, as well as the fact that saying a word while looking at it increases your chances of spotting mistakes. Have your trusty blue, red, or wild purple pen on hand and dive right in. This first read through will find the glaring errors, but there will still be more lurking in there without any doubt.

You Say What?!

I admit that it took me a while to appreciate the value in this next tip, but I promise you that it really works, even though it can sometimes make your eyeballs feel just a tiny bit wobbly. Here, what you need to do is to read your manuscript backwards. At this point you'll have corrected all the errors that you've found so far on your computer, so now you're looking for new ones. Go to the very last page of your book and read it word by word. I know that this may seem a little bit like torture, and obviously you don't have to do any of the things suggested here, but this truly is the most outstanding way to confuse that little you inside you who knows what should be there next. Looking at the words individually takes the story away. In fact if you decide to apply only one of these proofreading tips to your work this is the one I would choose. Yes it will take you longer this way than reading from front to back, but you'll have a better shot at spotting those gremlins.

Oy, I need a Holiday

Have another couple of days away from your manuscript. I generally take two days doing something else – or not very much as the case may be. This next bit could actually seem like fun if you're publishing for the very first time. Here you should download Kindle for PC and transform your rough manuscript into a MOBI file using Calibre as described in the Converting Your Manuscript section – don't worry about formatting or general appearance, just convert it as it is now. Whether or not you prefer reading your eBooks on an actual Kindle or other device, Kindle for PC is a wonderful tool for proofing, and absolutely vital to have as a self publisher. We'll see later how important it is to view your published book on as many reading devices that you possibly can to be sure that your readers don't have a nasty reading experience, but for now, we'll see how handy it is for proofing.

Once you've created a MOBI file, double click on the little blue book icon, and it will open in your Kindle for PC. This book will give you a totally different reading experience from what you would get reading the manuscript on your computer or paper, and another opportunity for spotting typos. Read the book through from front to back.

Is the End Nigh? Oh Please Say it is.

Almost done now scribblers. Gird your loins and do another spell check on your computer. If you've added or changed any text, there could be brand new typos in there. Double check your names using the Find tool in Word. If you've changed a character's name at any point in your book there could be some proper howlers waiting to confuse your readers. Also if you use a name with multiple spellings like Laurence and Lawrence it is a good idea to check. Use this same tool to check for words you know that you commonly overuse – like really or just – two of my own. Take your time checking the your and you're, its and it's, and other known offenders. You should have a pretty clean manuscript by now. Print it out again and repeat step two.

Proofreader

You can now format it (or pay for outsourced formatting, but remember, if you make changes later you may have to pay for this again – best to have a go and try yourself first), and then send it for proofreading if you can afford it, and choose to make use of this service. Many authors choose only to use proofreaders, and edit their books themselves, so that's entirely your decision. Make sure that you get what you pay for. These services can be very expensive, so check credentials, references, and recommendations before making your choice.

Swopsies

If you can't afford proofreading then you could try swopping the service for payment in kind, or for something else that you are good at. The Indie world is full of truly wonderful people. Writers published, and not yet published support each other in many ways. It goes without saying that having another author proofread your work is all good. Either swop for the same, or offer some other help with some aspect of publishing that you're better at. Like cover design if you're creative.

Is This Really the End?

Probably not. Even if you hire a proofreader as well as following these steps yourself, typos have a habit of sneaking through. The great thing is that whenever a typo rears its ugly head at some point in the future, it's really easy to fix, and to reload to Amazon and CreateSpace without losing any of your reviews. Even if there are still a couple in there, you'll eventually get to zap all of those little lurgies as you find them.

Beta Readers

If you are going to have people beta read your book, then send the manuscript out to them after your own initial edit and proofing, but before sending it to your paid for editor or proofreader. I have to admit that I've haven't yet used beta readers myself, but so many other authors I know have only the greatest of praise for them, so while I personally haven't used them, I think they're great anyway, and plan on using them in the future. I do beta read the books of author friends, and it really is a great experience reading a book before it's published, so there honestly is no shame in asking. They can also pick up any lurking typos and grammar gremlins with a bit of luck. If you're new to publishing and haven't yet been exposed to the very different things readers like or don't like about any given book, be prepared for this now, and analyse feedback carefully. Don't get cross or defensive. These readers are only trying to help. At the same time, don't rush to change something about your book that you're very happy with unless all of your beta readers have a problem with it, and even then, the decision must ultimately be yours.

Critique Groups and that Facebook Guy

Oh, and just in passing. Beware of those people who just love to rip the words of others apart. Make sure that you trust those people you ask to critique your book if that's a route you decide to go. There are some out there who seem to get a great deal of pleasure tearing down the work of new writers whether they're asked to or not. On one occasion when I was still a total newbie, one of those dreadful armchair literati completely rewrote a short story of mine without any invitation to do so, and then sent it to me. Luckily his interpretation was horribly ridiculous and gave me no more than a great chuckle, or I might have just given up writing entirely. Believe in yourself, and wait for your readers opinions without letting the hypercritical lurker trolls get you down.

Make a Copy or Two

Before we move on to the formatting stages, make at least one copy of your final manuscript. The formatting for your paper book is different to the formatting for your eBook, and if you later decide to publish on any other bookselling platform it will be best to format specifically for each different site. Send a copy of your clean manuscript to yourself via email, and also keep it stored on a device other than your computer for safety's sake.

PUBLISH ON AMAZON

Make new folders for each platform that you intend to publish on. One for Amazon Kindle and another for your paper book on CreateSpace, and put a new copy of your finished manuscript into each.

Formatting for Kindle is a simple process, and the concept of less is more rules. You don't want any fancy formatting that could corrupt your book file. Never use multiple spaces or individually indent your paragraphs with your tab key. Leave that tab key alone in general. If you have already done this, use the Show/Hide (the pilcrow ¶ symbol) function to show formatting and remove all of them, as well as any other unnecessary fancy formatting. Click on the symbol in the top ribbon of your word document and you'll be able to see all formatting marks, then you can go through your manuscript and delete as necessary. You could also remove all the formatting in your book and start from scratch by highlighting and selecting the whole document, then clicking on the downward facing arrow beneath the Change Styles box and then clicking on Clear All. Unless you have quite a lot of unwanted formatting, the first method should be good enough though. Clearing all formatting means going through your manuscript again and redoing all of it.

I suggest inserting a few pages for your front matter using section breaks. Go to Page Layout and select Breaks from the Page Setup box, and then format your manuscript. The reason for section breaks rather than the page breaks we use between chapters is that you can use different formatting in each section, whereas with page breaks it all has to be the same. It's a good idea to use the Look Inside feature on Amazon to see the front matter of a couple of bestsellers. They're not all the same but they all look neat and professional. That's the look you want to go for. Centre your book title and author name on the title page, and centre or justify anything else you decide to put in the front of your book. The copyright page (also centred) comes after the title page and then everything else is after that. The front section of your book is vitally important. Potential readers must not be able to differentiate it from any bestseller when they look inside, so spend as much time as you need to getting the front spot on.

I like to put the blurb in the front matter of my books with the About this Book heading. This isn't a common practice but I found that I have so many books on my Kindle that I forget what they were about and end up passing them by time and again rather than heading back to Amazon to find out, so this is a nice reminder.

Keep in mind that the amount of content in your front matter will affect how much of your book potential readers will get to see in the Look Inside feature on Amazon. They might not buy it if they can't see a sample of the writing style, so if you do decide to add reviews or anything else to the front of your book, try and calculate how much space it will take.

You can add a dedication or preface, and some authors add an About the Author page as well. I prefer to add that to the back of my books to free up more Look Inside space.

Formatting Your Book

Go to the Page Layout tab in the top ribbon above your document, and click the little arrow to the right of the Paragraph selection. Select Indents and Spacing and change Special to First Line, and then change By to your preferred size of paragraph indent. The standard indent size is 0.5 but you can choose the size you prefer. Some authors use 0.3. Some authors don't indent at all. Again I suggest using that Look Inside feature to see how the top selling books are formatted to decide what layout you like.

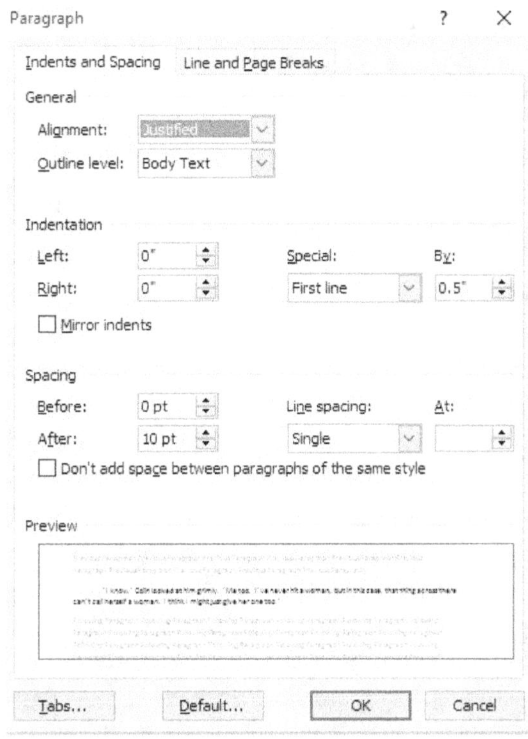

In the same box, set your automatic Spacing, which is the spacing left between paragraphs, to your desired size, and set line spacing to Single.

Insert Page Breaks before each new chapter.

There are no numbers on the pages of Kindle eBooks, so don't insert headers, footers and page numbers.
Kindle only uses seven basic fonts, and readers can change them according to their preference. They can also change the font size, so selecting 12pt and using a simple font like Times New Roman or Garamond is a safe choice.

Check that all the links within your book and also to online sites or other published books are clickable, using Ctrl Click while hovering over each one. To create a clickable link, type out the words that will be seen, such as the title of a book or the name of a website. Highlight that text, and right click on it. Select Hyperlink from the box that opens, paste the link URL into the little text box, and click OK. The text will now be blue and clickable. To link within your book, highlight the text you want to link do the same but choose a place in the document. There are detailed instructions on how to do this in the Table of Contents section.
If you're using images in your book, make sure that there are no paragraph indents to the left of them, or this could chop off the right hand side of them when viewed on Kindle. Also, don't use any Microsoft Word generated graphics or pictures and screenshots without first converting them to JPEG or your chosen image format, and then using the Insert Picture function. Never copy and paste an image into a manuscript destined to become an eBook. Under the Make Your Own Cover section of this book, you'll see how to download the free Paint.net software. If you do want to use any charts or tables and clipart from word you must first convert them to images to insert. Here's how to do that easily with Paint.net.

Take a screenshot of your image using the Print Screen key on your keyboard. You'll see the little image on your clipboard.

Open Paint.net.

Click on Edit in the top ribbon.

Select Paste Into New Image and crop it as necessary.

Save As JPG or to the format you require.

There are also many online tools that you can use to resize and manipulate images with, but I find it much easier to have the software on my computer ready to use at any time.

Create Table of Contents

This is the one part of the self-publishing process that made me want to pull my hair out in bunches to begin with. Right now, a NCX (Navigation Control File) table of contents is mandatory when you publish with Amazon. Some self-publishers use KindleGen and Sigil, while others swear by Scrivener. Unfortunately these had my eyes crossed in minutes, and there really isn't a lot of easily accessible online help available that is comprehensible to anyone not versed in HTML coding. Luckily I found a much simpler and reliable way which I'll share with you.

There are two types of table of contents that we need to know about as self-publishers. The logical clickable table and the NCX table. The first is the visible one in the front matter of your eBook (sometimes in the back matter), and the second is a hidden HTML table of contents which ensures that your table of contents is live in your book's Go To menu. If that sounds confusing to you as a writer, rather than a computer programmer, there's no need for shame. This has proven to be the most head-scratching part of formatting for me, and the one thing that has taken the most research and trial and error to learn.

The truth is that unless you do understand how to write HTML coding, it's not something that you're going to be able to do on your own. You can outsource this part of your book preparation to a professional, or you can do it yourself using Calibre and Amazon's Kindle Previewer. I loaded most of my eBooks on to Amazon as MOBI files generated by Calibre, and they all have working and clickable NCX tables of contents in their Go To menus, but Amazon has updated their list of acceptable files, stating that while all the other formats are still fine to load, only MOBI files generated by their own software will be accepted. This is quite easy to do once you've followed the steps below, as you'll see in the Converting Your Manuscript section.

How to Create the Table of Contents

This process will create your Logical Table of Contents that will appear in the front matter of your book, and also what is needed for Calibre to produce a book with the NCX file. First of all forget all the heading styles. We're going to stick to Normal Style for chapter headings for this. It makes no difference if you centre them or align left – whatever your preference will be fine.

Choose a page for your book's table of contents. The one directly after the copyright page is the one commonly used.
Type the words Table of Contents and then type out your chapter heading names or numbers beneath that.

The next step is to bookmark each chapter heading in the book individually. Go through your book and highlight them one by one, and from the Insert tab select Bookmark. Type in your bookmark name without using spaces, for instance, chap1 for chapter one, then click Add. When you've done this for all chapter headings, return to your typed out table of contents, highlight the words Table of Contents and insert a bookmark called toc.

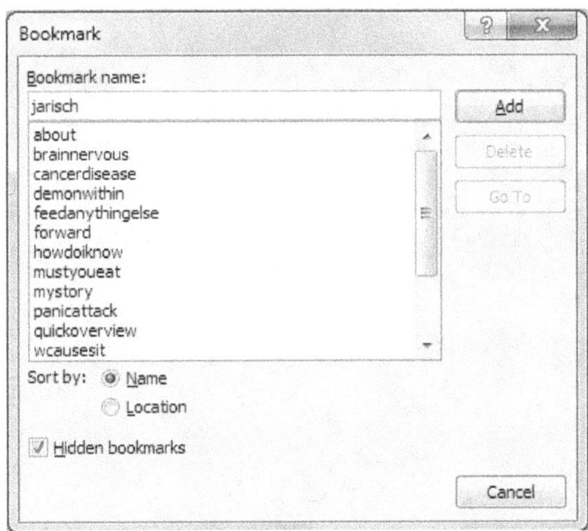

To link them, go back to your typed out table of contents, highlight your first chapter heading, right click and select Hyperlink from the insert tab. Choose “Place in the document”, click on its associated bookmark and click OK. Then repeat this process with each chapter.

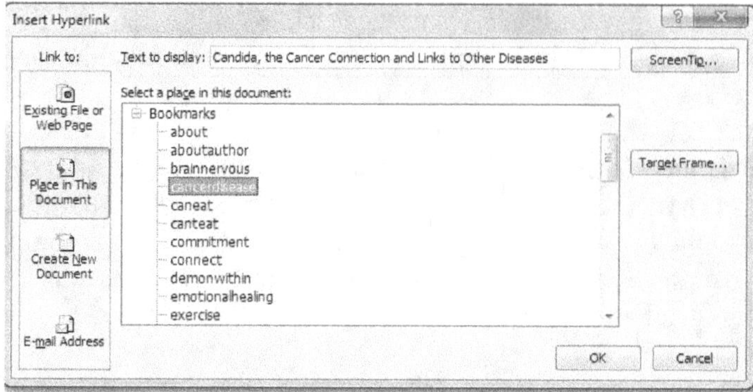

What you need to do next is to link your chapters back to the table of contents in the other direction. Hover over your chapter headings one by one and press Ctrl on your keyboard and then left click your mouse, which will take you to the relevant chapter heading in the body of the book. Highlight the heading, and then select Insert and then Hyperlink and click on the bookmark named toc.

Word creates a lot of hidden bookmarks which need to be deleted rather than risk them messing with your formatting. To do this, click on Insert and then Bookmarks. You’ll see a little box labelled “Hidden Bookmarks”. Click on that and go through the list, removing all of those that you haven’t put in there yourself. Click on each of them and then use the Delete button in the box to get rid of them. And you’re done. Save and move on to the next step.

CREATING YOUR COVER

We've all seen some pretty toe curling cover art. Even though there are some downright awful cover images out there, I believe that it is the typography that can make or break a book's face. Your book's cover is vitally important. A cover that looks sloppy or amateurish is not going to gain you readers no matter how wonderful your words are. Not everyone has the natural ability to create the cover that they see in their mind's eye, but the cost of bespoke cover art is often not affordable to everyone, and that's sometimes when Indies can get it wrong because they don't know what other free options are available to them. A lot of writers are also extremely creative with oodles of artistic flair though, and with the right tools can make fantastic cover designs for themselves and others if they want to. They just need the tools for the job which is what we'll get into next.

As I said, if you can afford it, you can buy an original design or illustration for your book from a cover artist, which will likely be the most expensive option. You can also buy a pre-made cover from one of many designers who use stock images they've purchased, or use their own artworks from other projects. Although the covers using purchased stock images can seem really reasonable, beware of duplications. It won't be nice to see your cover on someone else's book, or worse yet, quite a few other books, and could lose you potential readers if they think they've already read it because of the familiar cover. Many cover designers simply tweak colours and aspects, whack on a fancy font, and Bob's your uncle – duplicates all over the place. I've also personally checked a couple only to find that the images on them have no licence anywhere to be found, which could mean that they were never loaded on to the internet for anyone other than their owner's pleasure. Possibly their owners don't really care if you use their image for your book cover without asking, but then again they very probably will. Also, it's illegal, so don't do that.

If you have zero cash in your cover budget and no artistic ability at all, I suggest first considering finding a creative Indie to swop services with, but if that fails and you're really on your own, read on.

Probably the easiest way to make one is to purchase and pay for a stock image from sites such as Dreamstime and Shutterstock – they're very reasonably priced, and then head over to a free to use online site such as Picmonkey or Canva to add your title and author name. You also have the option of using Amazon's Cover Creator.

By paying for an image you shouldn't have to worry about the rules that sometimes can make the use of an unchanged free image illegal, but even so, always carefully read the licence of the image you're purchasing. Often, editorial images which are fine to purchase for use on blogs and articles are not licensed for commercial use from some stock image sale sites. Don't ever use a free image of a person. Not even a portion of a person if there's a remote chance that anything in it could be recognisable by them. If you want pictures of people on your cover, you must always pay for them, unless you can obtain a signed model release. This applies to pictures of certain buildings as well. Many of the free image sites listed in this book have photos that you are allowed to do anything you like with, but there are a couple that require their free images to be changed. You can't use them exactly as they are for your cover. That's not a bad thing in this case, because you want your cover design to be as original as you can make it. Always have a look at a free image site's terms of use policy, so you know what you can do with your chosen images.

If you already have and know how to use Photoshop or Gimp or one of the many other design choices out there, then you're halfway there, but if you don't have a design programme, have never used one, and can't afford to pay for one, never fear. There are quite a few free resources out there. Gimp is free but I have never used it, so I'm going to show you my absolute favourite free programme. These days I have a couple of excellent design programmes on my computer as well as the online paid for ones, but this freebie was my first, and I still use it all the time. It's a wonderful tool to keep, and there are loads of tutorials for various projects using it on YouTube if you're interested in using it for other things.

I'm going to assume though, that you're a writer who has absolutely no knowledge of or interest in digital or any other kind of art creation, and I'm going to show you only the exact steps and processes that you need to know to put your cover together.

The Equipment

Download Paint.net and install it.
Also download their Megalo Effects plugin.

The Vision Board

What do you want your cover to look like? Grab a pencil and paper and draw a rough sketch. Look around online and see if any images out there inspire you. Your book has taken hundreds of hours of your life to make it as good as it can be. Let's give it a face to be proud of. Once you have your vision board for what you would like to see on your cover, let's get all the elements together.

Where to Look?

How about your own photos? The smartphones of today take excellent high quality photos, or you could use your camera to take some shots to use for your cover. Think outside of the box, and you'll be amazed at the things all around you that could make for a great cover design. You could set up a photo shoot in your home. For instance, a high heeled shoe and a glass of red wine positioned on crumpled satin, or a rose and jewellery on black velvet. A photo of a sports car (registration number not visible), or maybe a corner of a beautiful garden. There are countless things around you that could be used for your cover, and you wouldn't have to worry at all about copyright.

If this idea doesn't appeal, then it's time to look around online for your cover artwork. You can purchase images from various sites online as I said, such as Dreamstime or Shutterstock, and there are also places where you can get stunning high resolution photographs free for commercial use, such as Unsplash and my favourite, Pixabay. You can use images from both of these sites either as they are, or you can change them as you desire without any concerns at all about copyright, and there really are some absolutely stunning pictures to choose from.

If you use images from other free sources, always look up their licences first. Some require attribution and some require that that their images can't be used as is, but are free to use if changed and manipulated. Also, some where you can download certain images for free, such as from Dreamstime, have restrictions to their use for commercial purposes. Make certain that you have no limit to the amount of books you can sell with the image on them as well.
Have a look at the different types of licence on Creative Commons so that you're confident that there can be no nasty surprises down the road. If an image has no licence at all then definitely don't use it.

Resolution, Size and Quality

The resolution of a picture is the pixels per inch. The higher the resolution, the higher the quality. Amazon require a minimum height/width rate for book covers of 1 000 pixels on the long side, and 625 pixels on the short side with a maximum of 10 000 pixels. Their suggested best quality is 2 500 pixels on the long side, but they'll accept anything between the minimum and the maximum.

While building the cover in Paint.net you are going to be working with layers, layering each component image on top of the previous one until you get your desired cover. The first image you load for the base of the cover must have a larger resolution than those to follow, so check your image sizes before starting. You could load any large sized image to begin with simply to get your base set up if your base image isn't bigger than the rest of the images that will go above it. I like to start with a base image of 3456 x 5184 and resize it down later. Amazon charges you fifteen cents per megabyte of your total book size for every one you sell, but that isn't much. Don't try and calculate this from your Word document size because the final MOBI file will be smaller, and you can see then how much you will pay.

Getting Started

If you feel that you don't have any artistic ability, then the first thing you have to do is look at covers on Amazon. Even if you are creative this is a great way to get a feel for how a book cover gets put together. Dissect covers that you like by their elements and fonts. Look at each part of them individually, and see how they came together. When you have an idea of what you'd like to see on your own cover then get started. A great cover is not the same as a beautiful painting in many ways. Cover creation is an art form of its own. The text and picture have to work together, and everything must be placed so that it becomes one without jarring the eye. Choosing the wrong font can sometimes ruin beautiful art. Now that you have an idea of what you want for your cover, and have collected your images, I'm going to go through exact steps using Paint.net to get the job done.
Open Paint.net

Firstly, for your peace of mind, check out the Undo icon – the backward pointing arrow just beneath the Adjustments tab. Paint.net allows you to go back and undo any number of actions, so don't worry if you make a mistake – just hit the Undo button if you do. Go slow with this if it's your first go around on design software, and don't stress. You'll get it right in the end.

In the top ribbon from left to right are your main commands. File, Edit and View first. Image is where you will go if you want to resize an image or flip or rotate it. Next is your Layers box. As you create your cover design, each new element that you want to add gets its own layer, so you will use Add New Layer from the Layers box before each one. Here you will also find the Import From File command, which allows you to browse your computer for your next image. There are many options in the Adjustment box, and you can play around with them if you want to, to see what they do. I mostly only use the Hue/Saturation adjustment here. Just click on it and you can change the colour of any image. The last one in the top strip is Effects. Paint.net has tons of effects as well as many more plugins to download for free. Again, I suggest you play with these for both images and fonts. There are instant chrome effects, flames and many others available.

In the upper left of the screen you'll see the Toolbox. I'm not going to show you how to use all of these tools – that would be a book in itself - only the ones I'll be using here to create a basic cover. Each and every one of them have exact and easy to follow instructions on Paint.net's website. Below that is the Colour Wheel. From here you'll select colours for your fonts or any artwork you design. In the bottom right corner is your Layers box. Here you can see where you are in your design. At the bottom right of the Layers box there is a Layer Properties icon. This is where you set the opacity for the layer you're working on, making it as see through as you'd like it. Have a look at Blending Mode in this same box, and see the different effects you can get when you change it.

If you're loading a base image simply for the sizing and don't want it to be visible, click on File > Open. Browse for this image and upload it. From the Layers box, select Add New Layer. Then click on the Fill icon (the little bucket), click on white in your colour box at the bottom left of your screen, and then click on the image. This will give you a clean white base. Add new layer. Click on Import From File in the Layers box and browse for your first image. Change hues or add effects and adjustments, and then add a new layer, and browse for your next image using Import From File.

Stretch out or shrink your new image to the size that you want it, and move it around until it's positioned where you want it to be. This is where we get to the useful little tools in the toolbox up there. I'll give you a brief overview of what the ones I've found helpful with cover design can do. Explaining the whole of Paint.net here would take up too much space in this book so I'll just cover the basics. You can get full and very easy to follow instructions on all of the tools on their website.

For your second image use a photo of any single item or creature with a simple background.

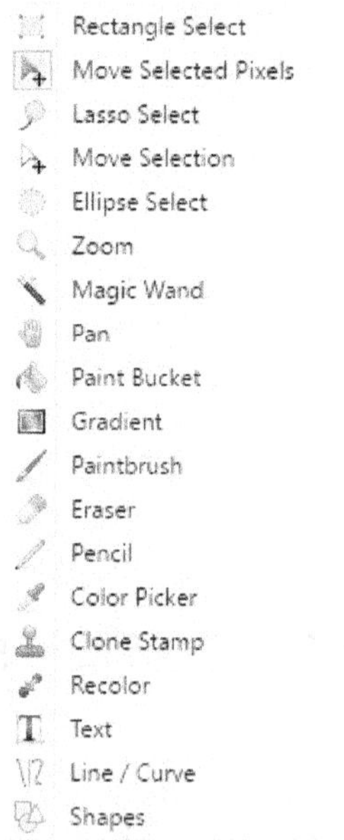

Click on Rectangle Select and select a small portion of your image, and then click on the icon of a pair of scissors in the top ribbon. You will see that the part you selected has been erased from the image on the second layer, and is showing the portion of the first image instead. Use this tool to remove rectangular shaped portions of any current image. You can stretch it to both sides of an image or from top to bottom. Press the Undo button to get back to your image. You can use the Lasso Select tool beneath it for the same thing for shapes. Now select the Magic Wand tool and the click on the background behind the item or animal. Wait for the dotted lines to appear and click on the little pair of scissors again. Either all of the background or most of it will have been erased. Now click on the Eraser and select Brush Width to get the most useful size from the top ribbon, and erase the portions of the background that are still there. It can be tricky to perfectly erase sections very close to an image. The thing to do then is to zoom in to enlarge which makes it much easier to get at the fiddly bits. Your first few attempts will not yield works of art, but with a little bit of practice you'll get it right. If the magic wand selects parts of the image to delete that you want to keep, add a new layer and paint around the image with a bright colour. The zoom function will come in handy here again. When you're done, save as JPEG, close, reopen, and use the magic wand again. Finally, click on the Layer Properties icon in the bottom right hand corner of the Layers box in the bottom right corner of your screen. Change the opacity and see the results you get, then try different blending modes to see how they work.

When your cover image is as you want it, you can either Merge Layers Down from the Layers box and then save, or you can select Save As from the File box in the top ribbon, and then name your image and select an image format, such as JPEG. Say yes when you're asked to flatten the image. This is the extra simple how to version. Look at Paint.net's tutorials for more on layers. You can add or remove as many layers as you like, and save your ongoing project if you don't complete it in one sitting, although I find it easier to save the actual image, no matter how far along it is to completion. It is important to save your cover design before you add your fonts in case you want to change anything later on.

When you're ready to add your book title and author name, there are quite a few free sites online such as Fontsquirrel that are easy to use and offer great fonts. Picmonkey is one of my favourite sites for applying text to covers, although Canva is also great if you don't want to work in layers with Paint.net. Cooltext is another useful free resource for titles and author names.

Open your cover image in Paint.net and add a new layer. Select the Text icon – third from the bottom in the toolbox. Select the font and font size from the top ribbon. Expand the colour box by pressing More. You will then have more options including opacity. Choose your font colour. Click on the image and type your book title. Now you can change fonts, size and colour and it will automatically change on your typography until you get the look and size that you want. You can also click on and drag the little box beneath the text and move it around. Once you're happy with the title, add a new layer and do the same for your author name. You can only use one font, size, and colour per layer, so make a new layer for each element. Look at the various font effects you can get from the Effects box in the top ribbon, and also try the different blend modes. I suggest saving as an image after each layer. You can delete them later on, but they can be useful along the way because you'll more than likely change your mind a few times. If the largest font size isn't big enough, just click into the size box and type in a higher value. One thing I would recommend is that you make a note of the names of the fonts you use for each particular cover, as well as the sizes and any effects you used in case of future changes.

When you're finally satisfied with your cover, save it as a JPEG image, and make a copy or two. It's a good idea to save copies of both the finished design and also the image before fonts were added. Also email it to yourself and store it on an external back up device.

As an example, here are the elements I used to make a simple sample cover. The first image is a photo I took of a wall, and then using the adjustments and gradient tools I changed the hue and colour.

Then I took another photo of a set of fireplace tools, and used it as my second layer, erasing the background with Paint.net as described above, and positioning it where I wanted. I then added a few bloody splotches using Picmonkey, as well as their comic book effect function.

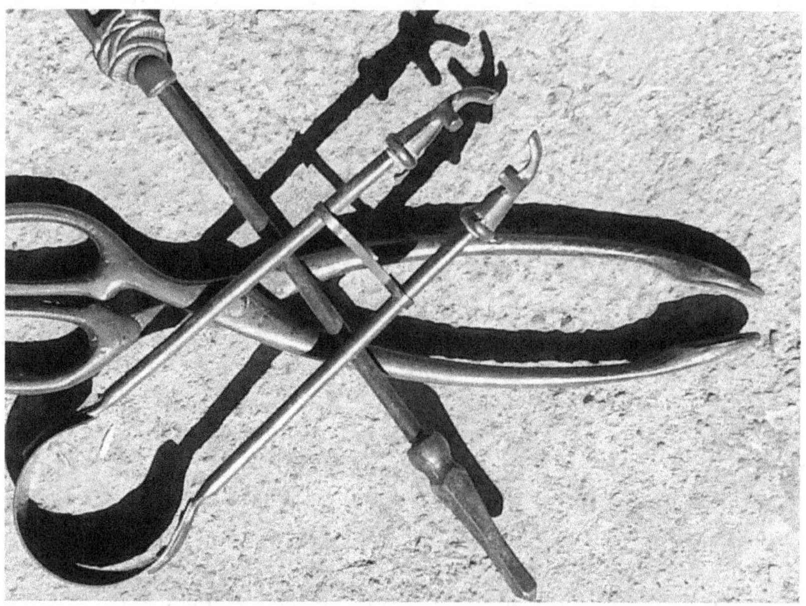

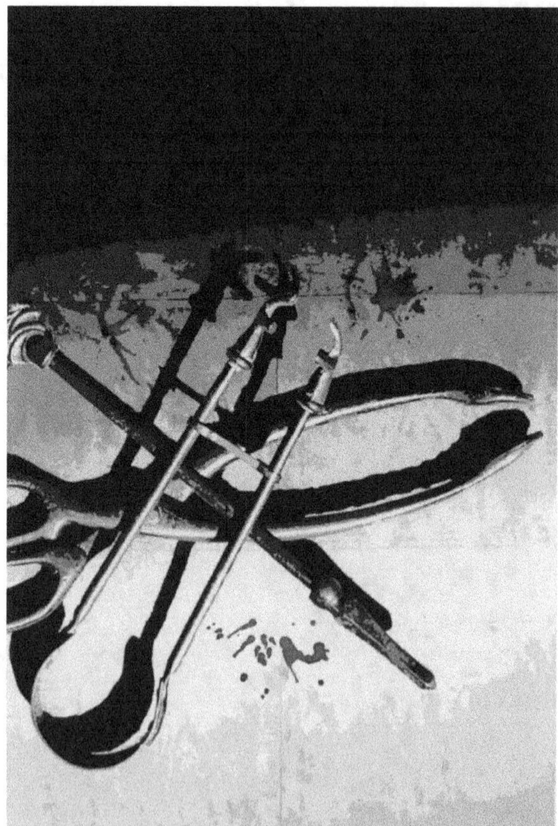

Finally I added layers for title and author, using simple and common fonts.

Obviously you don't have to take your own photos if you don't want to. Use any of the free to use images you find that you like on the sites that offer them. Making a cover won't take you ten minutes, and it shouldn't. Covers I create for myself as well as those I sell to other authors can take days or longer depending on how much effort they need put into them. It's definitely something you can do if you take the time. It's worth it.

Free fonts are available for you to download online from various sites. When you see one that you like simply download it. Open the file you've downloaded and read the text first. Fonts also have usage licences, and sometimes they require attribution even though they're free. Don't ever use any font that has a licence you don't understand, or requires attribution unless you're prepared to place that attribution wherever you use it. I haven't wanted one badly enough yet to consider a font attribution in any of my books, so I delete those, or pay for them so that I don't have to use attribution. There are more than enough great fonts to use without concern of accidental thievery. If they are free to use then click on install and they will appear for you to use both in your Word font collection and on Paint.net.
Look for free images to use for your designs on Unsplash, Pixabay, Public Domain Pictures, Splitshire, 1 Million Free Pictures, Wikipedia, and Public Domain Archive.

CONVERTING YOUR MANUSCRIPT

Calibre is free to download software that you can use as a library for your collection of eBooks, but most importantly it converts your finished manuscript into either MOBI or ePub formats. The formats that Amazon accepts include Word (DOC or COCX), HTML, MOBI, ePub, Rich Text Format, Plain Text, Adobe PDF and Kindle Package Format, although Amazon has updated this list with the proviso that they will only accept MOBI files made with Amazon software. You have the choice of loading the Calibre generated ePub straight up on to Amazon, or you can generate a MOBI file using Amazon's Previewer software, which is my own chosen method. When you load an ePub file into the Previewer it then generates a MOBI file using KindleGen, and this is the file that you should use to upload.

Converting Your Manuscript with Calibre

Now that you're happy with your completed manuscript and ready to let it loose, firstly save it and make a copy, then save it as an HTML document. Don't save as HTML without saving the Word document first. This is easily done by clicking Save As, then Other Formats, and selecting Web Page, Filtered from the drop down menu. A warning will pop up about losing formatting which is nothing to worry about. Select save anyway. You will see that you now have two manuscripts of the same name – one a word document and another HTML. You can actually load this HTML document straight on to Amazon, but the NCX table of contents isn't guaranteed this way, which is why I recommend the following method.

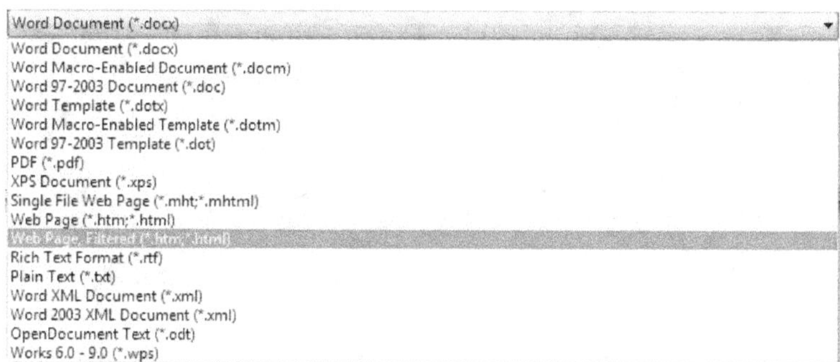

Download and install Calibre and open it. I suggest having a quick look at the manual, and having a look at the various functions. It's a simple and useful bit of software to have. Click on the Add books icon in the top left of your screen, and then browse for and select the HTML file of your book. Choose ePub as the output format in the top right hand corner. If you want to create your own Kindle books at a later stage, you'd select MOBI, and add a cover by clicking on the icon beneath the gold one and browsing for your own. Then select Convert books (third from the left), and a new screen will appear for your metadata. Fill in the book's title and your author name.

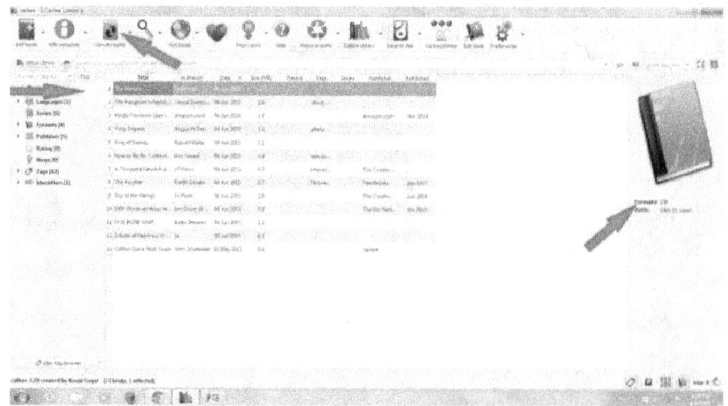

Go to the Table of Contents box on the left, and select Force Table of Contents. Click OK.

You'll see a turning circle at the bottom of the screen while Calibre converts your book. When it's ready the cover will appear in the panel on the right. Beneath it you will see your author name, and beneath that Formats: Either ePub or MOBI, Zip and Path: Click to Open. Select Click to Open and it will take you to your book's folder in your Calibre library.

When you make MOBI files for your own purposes, click on the little blue MOBI book icon, and it will open up in your Kindle for PC.

Open your Kindle Previewer. Select Open Book and browse for your ePub by going to the Calibre Library folder that will have been created in your My Documents library. Double click on the ePub file of your book.

Wait a short time, and then it will tell you that your book has been created using KindleGen and provide you with a link to it. This MOBI file is now saved in the folder that was created in your Calibre library for your ePub. If you click OK you can view your book as it will be seen on Kindle devices, as well as check that your NCX table of contents is working. Go to the MOBI file in your Calibre library and double click on it, and it will open in your Kindle for PC for you to review there as well. This Kindle Previewer generated MOBI file is what you will load on to Amazon when you publish.

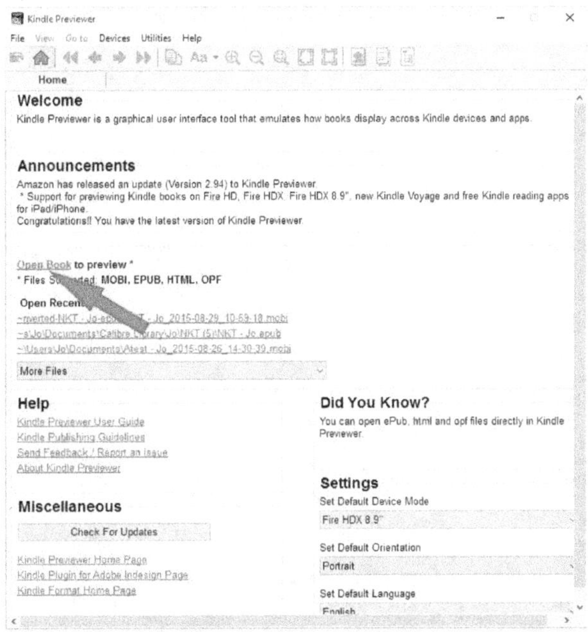

PUBLISHING ON AMAZON

Open your account at Amazon, and fill in all the required fields. If you don't live in the USA you have a couple of tax options, including allowing Amazon to withhold tax until you get around to getting to the proper processes. You can still publish and earn royalties until you do, and any withheld taxes will be paid to you when the necessary information is submitted, but the withheld amount is thirty percent so you might want to submit what is needed as soon as possible. Only certain countries are eligible to receive royalty payments by electronic fund transfer, otherwise Amazon will only issue paper cheques every time you accrue one hundred dollars. You do have another option though by using Payoneer which works very well. Register with them and they will send you a pay as you go credit card. When you receive this card, activate it on your online Payoneer account, and you will be issued with a United States cheque account. Fill in those account details for payment on your Amazon account, and your royalties will be deposited as they arrive. You can use this card as any other credit card in your own country.

You have the option of supplying your own purchased ISBN number or you can choose for Amazon to supply your book a free ASIN number.

Before you start the publishing process, being pre-prepared will make the process painless. Have your book description ready to go, as well as your planned categories and tags. The description will take you a while to write. Those little things can be deceptively difficult to get down, and your two categories and seven tags need to be properly researched rather than being picked as you go along. You can change categories and tags at any time, but choosing these is important to your book's discoverability, so look at books on Amazon in the same genres as yours for ideas. It's not necessary to repeat things. For instance, if your book's title is How to Grow African Violets, you don't need to use that in your tagging. Amazon will pick it up anyway in searches. Tags can be more than one word, and they are divided by commas, so make use of every one.

Is your book a serial or a series? Technically, serials have a tendency to end on cliffhangers, while books in a series should be able to be read as a complete book with a satisfying ending. Personally I'm partial to a good cliffhanger if it makes me think. I don't mind a cliffhanger in a standalone story if it's clear that it's there for a purpose, but that's just me. A cliffhanger is one thing that can get right up many a reader's nostrils, and cause them to make the pain of not knowing what happens next go away by leaving one star scorchers. There are very popular serials on Amazon, but they are clearly and visibly labelled, so you can publish them without fear of being stomped on, as long as you make sure that you aren't labelling serials as series.

Once your account is set up, go to your bookshelf and click on Add Book. Slowly complete all the fields. It's a very easy process, and if at any point you're not sure, there are little "What is this?" boxes next to everything.

Decide whether or not to set Digital Rights Management. Once this is set on any particular book it can't be changed, so be sure of your choice. If you do set it on any particular book, then that book cannot be lent out or changed into any other reading format. If you don't then it can be converted to ePub or any other format, and the purchaser can choose to lend it out.

Set your pricing at what the regular price is going to be for your book, and not for a lower price that you maybe are planning to use to get early sales rolling. Set the price at 3.99 if that's what you want to sell it for generally, and then after it goes live go back and change it to 0.99 cents for your promotion period. That way the slashed through selling price is clearly seen on your book page above the promotional price. For any book priced below US$2.99 you only have the option of choosing a thirty five percent royalty although Amazon doesn't charge per megabyte delivery on these, and for US$2.99 to US$9.99 you get to choose the seventy percent royalty. There is no reason to choose the lower royalty here. Obviously, what you sell your book for is entirely up to you, but it's probably not going to sell much if it's priced the same as a Stephen King. You don't want to sell it too cheaply either. Setting a fair price to it and then occasionally discounting it is a much better idea. Unless you have a specific reason not to want to sell your book in certain territories, set them for worldwide distribution.

If you decide to use a pen name for whatever reason it isn't a difficult process. You must open your account using all of your real details, but that isn't publicly shown unless you want it to be. Simply publish the book as always with the only difference being that you enter your pen name in the author section. That's the only name to go there. Don't put your real name in any of those boxes. Once the book goes live, find it and claim it. A little box will come up asking if your name is misspelled or if you are using a pen name. Click on Let us know and you will then be allocated different Author Central pages for all the names you use, which you can toggle between from the top of your main Author Central page. Amazon supplies different author pages for up to three pen names per author, and nobody but you and Amazon will ever know who you really are if you don't want them to.

Your book file and cover file get loaded separately, both very simple processes. Upload straight from your computer, and wait to be told that each upload is successful. Click on Upload Book, browse, select the MOBI file that you created with the Amazon Previewer and upload. Do the same with your JPEG cover image. As soon as you see Upload and Conversion Successful, you get various options to review. I always download the MOBI preview file to go through on my Kindle for PC as well as paging through the online reviewer. Amazon also let you know if they find any possible errors in your book so always check those. Once you're happy, click Save and Publish. Your book will then be live on Amazon within the next twelve hours or so. Set up your Author Central page, and find and claim your book when you get the email informing you that it's live.

What are KDP Select and Kindle Unlimited?

There are quite a few authors who don't like these very much, but for a newbie they could very well be essential. If you sign a book up for KDP Select, you can't sell or publish the digital eBook anywhere else. You can opt out at any time, but there is a three month joining period each time, so you have to wait until any given three month segment has ended before you load it up on any other book selling site. Many first time Indie publishers are keen to get their books visible to the maximum number of possible readers, and it is really great to see your books on many different sellers, so it's easy to see why they don't opt in to Select.

From my own experience I suggest leaving your first book on KDP select at least for the first three months. Brand new books by first time authors are most likely to get their biggest sales on Amazon, and the benefits of Select can really help newly published authors.

Let me put it this way. It is very unlikely that the very first eBook you self-publish is going to put you in the position where you are going to be losing much money by not being allowed to have your book up for sale anywhere other than on Amazon. Authors who are a little more established, with a couple of books already out there for the past few years, maybe could feel financial pain this way, but they are not in the majority. Other than my first in a series novel, I haven't yet offered any of my full length books for free. In fact, two of them were not in KDP Select straight out of the gates because I wanted to have them on offer with Smashwords, Apple, and all the rest. Not too long ago I decided to unpublish them everywhere other than on Amazon, and see how the Select perks worked for me. Short answer is that I've made more money with Kindle Unlimited since then than I made from all of the other sites for the duration of the time that my books were offered there.

Kindle Select isn't a forever contract. It's a three month at a time deal, and not at all difficult to get out of if you decide that you want to sell your eBooks elsewhere at a later date. For me personally, getting my books down from all the Smashwords affiliated sites took much longer than that, and required that I had to scour all the related sites for them myself regularly to check that they were down before I could enrol them in Select. If you're self-publishing your first book, enrol the eBook into KDP Select for the first three month period before looking further afield. While it is rather gratifying to see it splashed around all over the place, you've got a lot bigger chance on making a "sale" with Kindle Unlimited as a new author, because if the reader doesn't like your book, they haven't lost anything other than their time. So while the dollar amount that you receive from the Unlimited "pool" might be less than what you would receive from an actual sale, it is still more than you'll receive from no sale at all.

Remember, KDP Select only applies to digital eBooks. Not your own digital audio book, and not paperbacks. You can offer those for sale anywhere you like.

Free Promotion Days

Every three months you get the opportunity to offer your book for free download for five days in total on KDP Select. You can use the five day block at one time or you can break it down and stagger the free days over the three month period. This is entirely a personal choice. The aim is to get your book read by people who would otherwise not be interested enough to pay for it. Then, hopefully, they'll love it and leave you a glowing review, and also buy any other books you may publish.

There are two diverging views on this is the Indie community. The first view is that it really is a great tool for the above reasons. This is actually true, and these free promotions offer even better value if you have multiple books out there. Give away the first in a series and you're very likely to sell some of the rest around the same time. The ratio of reviews received from giveaways compared to the books downloaded is generally very small, but the sooner your book has reviews the better.

The other opinion about these promotions is that there are so many millions of free eBooks floating around that people don't have to ever go to the trouble of buying any. This is true too, although the percentage of people who only ever download the free is a lot smaller than those readers who prefer to pay for what they really like and want. The freebie only people aren't going to pay for any books no matter what you do with yours, so I wouldn't worry about them at all. Most readers both pay for books and also download any freebies that catch their attention. I've often bought more books by an author I found out about from a free book. The other problem some authors have had with offering their books this way are some pretty awful reviews. Some people will download free things, very often not even checking to see if it's something they like, and then months later finding it on their Kindle, they read it, hate it, probably think they paid for it, and zap a one star stinker on Amazon for all to see. Maybe it was a genre they usually don't like but zooming through downloaded it on impulse.

I offer certain of my books free occasionally (mainly short stories) and others have never been free at this point, even though they are on KDP. They're there not particularly so that I can use them for free promotions, but for the other benefits.

Kindle Unlimited

For a fixed monthly sum, Kindle Unlimited subscribers can borrow any books in the programme, and all KDP Select books are. The authors of the borrowed books then get a share of the pot of subscription payments according to how many of their book's pages have been read. For bestselling authors who have their books selling at $9.99 and above this would mean losing quite a chunk out of their earnings because the KU dividends per book are generally less than the usual royalty. For brand new Indies the opposite is true. Readers are more willing to download a book by an unknown author this way, so even if you only get fifty percent of your actual sale royalty, it is money you would otherwise probably not have at all. It counts as a sale for your rankings, could earn you a nice review, and the possibility exists that you now have a new fan. Unless you're selling a lot of books anyway, Kindle Unlimited is a great benefit to new authors.

The beauty of being an Indie author is that you get to make all the decisions, and you can change your mind at any time if you want to place your books for sale elsewhere.

Pre-order

You can have your new book available on Amazon for pre-order for up to ninety days before the publication date. You do have to submit your draft manuscript for review, and that should be pretty complete with maybe only editing and proofing still to do. Even though the book isn't available for sale yet, it will still have a landing page where customers can order it, and they will only be charged once it goes live.

Kindle Countdown

Your book must be enrolled in KDP Select for you to make use of the Kindle Countdown, and priced between $2.99 and $24.99. It must have been enrolled in KDP for thirty days, and it must not have had its price reduced for that same period. Readers love bargains so this is also a really wonderful tool for Indies.

Also from Amazon

If you write non-fiction textbooks, books for children, or are a comic artist, have a look at Amazon's free software especially for creating these things. Kindle Textbook Creator, Kindle Kid's Book Creator, and Kindle Comic Creator.

Review

Always review on Kindle for PC. Even if the thought of reading books on your computer makes you cringe, it is important to view your book on as many possible readers as you can. There are actually quite a lot of people who love reading on their computer screens. Some can't afford to buy a Kindle, while others prefer the lovely big text there. I often read on my Kindle for PC for pleasure as well as for doing my work. Recipe books and how to books are at their very best on it, as are any books with images. I use it for research purposes, with specific libraries to hold reference books and materials. This way, forgetting or losing anything you collect for your writing doesn't happen often.

Also always review on Amazon's Kindle Previewer. Even though you have already reviewed the MOBI copy generated from your ePub, it's important to review again after the Amazon conversion. It's also a must have for when you update your books at a later stage, especially when you change a cover. You can go through your newly downloaded MOBI review file once again, without having to try and open it on your Kindle for PC which still has the old book file in it.

Publish

Once you've reviewed your files and are happy with your final book, push Save and Publish and continue. Your eBook should be live for sale within forty eight hours. Buy a copy of your book. Get friends and family to buy copies too, even if they won't be reading the eBook version. The more early sales you get, the better for its ranking.

Your Author Central Page (or Pages)

Set up your Author Central page with your bio, photo, and links to your Twitter feed and blog. Your books will be available for sale in more than just your country of residence, and you can set up your author page on each relevant Amazon site. You have to do each county's page individually if that's what you want to do, because your home Author Central page doesn't automatically show up everywhere.

Amazon's Review Policy

I personally prefer to let reviews for my books happen when they do, so I haven't actually asked for one yet. Reviews are important though so there is no harm in approaching book reviewers. Don't ever pay for them, unless you are paying what Amazon calls a professional reviewer. I don't believe that there is any sort of proof of what makes a reviewer professional, but I believe that they are referring to places like Kirkus or industry professionals. If you receive a gift certificate for a book in exchange for a review (especially if the gift certificate is for an amount higher than the price of the book) Amazon will view this as a paid for review and remove it when they see it unless you are actually a book reviewer. Definitely do read their guidelines on reviews so as to be safe.

If you have had any part in the creation of any book, you're not allowed to review it, except as an editorial review, which you can post on the book's landing page via Author Central. Reviews posted in the discussions thread right at the bottom of the landing page are allowed from anyone, including your family, but friends and family are not allowed to post actual reviews. There is no point in trying to buck the system, and if anyone does they will eventually get found out, and then lose their reviews anyway.

FORMAT & PUBLISH ON CREATESPACE

Now to get started on your paper book. First set up your account at CreateSpace. Log on here and set up your account. Fill in all your relevant details. As with Amazon, only certain countries are eligible for royalty payments to be made by direct deposit, so if you live in one that isn't you're going to receive payment by cheque. As I mentioned before for Amazon, Payoneer is another option to look into, because speaking from experience those cheques get large chunks taken out of them with bank fees, and they also take a while to clear.

Before you publish your book with CreateSpace you must consider what you want it to look like, because once the book has been assigned its ISBN number and is published you can't change the size of it or the colour of the paper. You can update the content and the cover later on though, so here just think a while on the size and paper. Grab a couple of books from your bookcase, measure them, and look at their interiors.

The default size on CreateSpace is six inches by nine inches, and the default paper colour is white. Traditionally published books generally have cream paper, apart from non-fiction which looks much better with white pages. My first two books are six by nine with white paper, which I can't change now, meaning that the rest of the books in my series are going to have to go with the same look. Now for my fiction I'm using cream paper and the five by eight inch size depending on the page numbers. Traditionally published books do use six by nine as well as other sizes. Consider how many pages are in your book when choosing the final size. Will it be a tall skinny tome, or a bulging smaller book?

Formatting for CreateSpace

You can download one of CreateSpace's free book interior templates and copy and paste your book into one, section by section, or you can format your book yourself. I've heard very positive opinions of the templates, but I've never used them myself. I have downloaded and had a look at them, and they seem straightforward enough to use, so you try that if the thought of any formatting at all has you trembling under the table. Otherwise, onward and forward to formatting from scratch, with one really easy first step.

If you're starting from a clean, unformatted manuscript this process should go easily for you if you follow the steps in succession. If you're working with an already formatted manuscript – meaning a document where you've set margins, indents, and so on as you like them, things could get a little tricky. Make sure that you have a couple of copies of your original manuscript. Have I already said that? Good. Until you have your final manuscripts to publish, you can never have too many copies, and even then you should have more than one of each. Clearing all formatting will remove every bit of formatting including fonts, justification, bold, italic, indents, and every other little thing, and it will mean that you'll have to dive in and redo all of this, checking carefully once you've got your page numbers in correctly. This might seem like hard work, but could save you quite a bit of torn out hair in the end, and give you a manuscript that is going to behave when it gets printed. You should do this if you have a huge amount of fancy formatting, such as space bar used for indents, or tabs. To clear all formatting, first select the whole document, then go to Home Tab > Styles > Clear All.

Page Numbers

The aim here is to have the page numbering begin from the first chapter of your book, with no page numbering before that. The very first thing to do with your CreateSpace manuscript is to number the pages. It's important to do this before any other formatting, because said formatting can really mess with your page numbers. In fact, trying to reformat any already formatted Word document is bound to throw you at least a few curve balls. Follow these steps in sequence and you should be fine though. I struggled for hours getting the page numbering right for my first books, but eventually had the very bright idea of making my own page numbering template, and then copying and pasting all my future manuscripts into that. I type my books without any formatting now, and then format them for Amazon and CreateSpace separately when they're done. Here's what to do. First, make your template for the page numbering of all your future books.

Open a new Word document.

Insert section breaks (not page breaks) after each page you'll need for your front matter up to and including the page before Chapter One begins. Or just insert three because you can always insert more later. Do this from the Page Layout tab, then Breaks and Next Page.

Then go to the page that is to be the first page of the first chapter and insert a page break using the Insert tab and selecting Page Break. From this point in the document, insert a page break after each chapter, and not a section break.

From the Insert tab, click on the little arrow at the bottom of the Page Number box to format. Insert > Page Number Arrow > Format Page Numbers. Select Start At 1 and click OK.

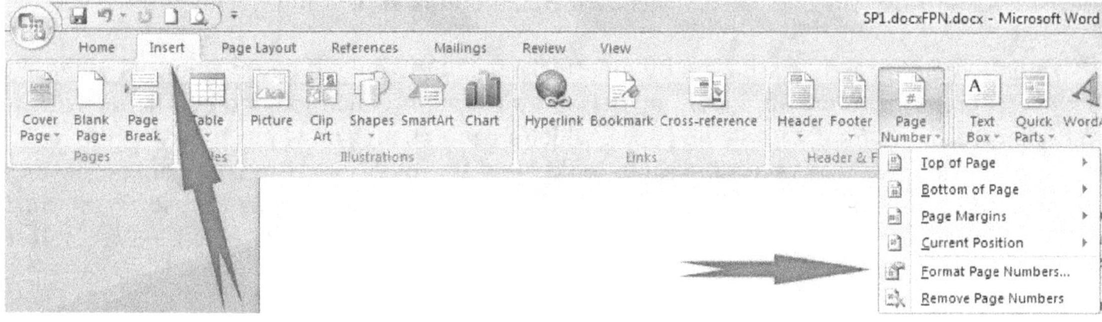

Still on the first page of your first chapter, and working backwards through your front matter, double click to open your headers and footers and unclick to remove all Link To Previous. Double click to close headers and footers. You don't want any Same as Previous on any of these pages.

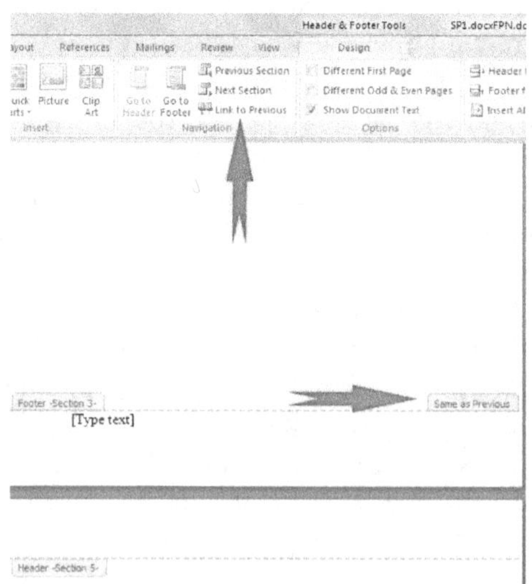

If you want your book title to show on every page from the first chapter, simply type it in the header. If you want your author name on the left pages and the title on the right hand pages, double click and go into the header of the first page of your first chapter. Select Different Odd & Even Pages and then type your name in the left header and your title in the right header. Go back and check that no Link to Previous boxes have reappeared, and if they have pop back into the relevant headers and footers and unclick them.

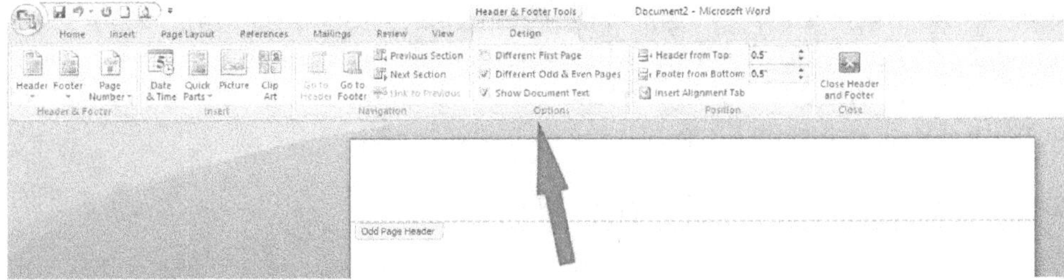

Finally, position your cursor in the footer of the first page of your first chapter and Insert > Page Numbers.

What should have happened now is that the first page number appears at the bottom of the second page of your first chapter, with no numbering on any of the pages of your front matter, and also not on the first page of your first chapter. The middle of the page is a nice place for the page numbers and headings in a book, but some authors prefer the right hand corner for numbers. Go to Page Layout > Page Setup Arrow > Pages and set the paper size to the size your book is going to be. Hit the Save button at this point before moving on and you now have your template.

Every time you're ready to publish with CreateSpace, copy and paste your whole manuscript into the first page of the first chapter, and then Save As > Book Title so you can keep your template as it is for future use. Then complete your front matter and finish formatting. This is the same process you use if you decide to try and add numbering to your whole already formatted manuscript. It's just a lot easier this way. If you are working with a completed manuscript rather than going with the template, insert a few section breaks in the beginning and follow the same process. If you add any more pages after formatting, then click in to headers and footers to check for and remove any new Link To or Same As Previous.

Be sure to use page breaks between chapters and never carriage returns. After the last sentence of your previous chapter, use Insert > Page Break.

Justify your text. I know that some authors choose not to justify text in their eBooks (not me), but a paper book really must be justified or it's going to look messy. Choose your font and font size. I like 12pt Times New Roman, but this is personal choice. I suggest again that you raid your bookshelf and see what you like in your collection.

By now you've decided on what trim size your book is going to be, so set your manuscript's size accordingly. From the Page Layout tab, click on the little arrow to the right of Page Setup, then select Paper from the three tabs at the top of the page setup box. Change the Width and Height settings to 6" x 9" or 5" x 8" or whatever size your book will be. If your book has images in it that extend to the edges of the pages, then add .125 to the width and .25 to the height. So you would then apply 6.125 and 9.25. Apply to Whole Document.

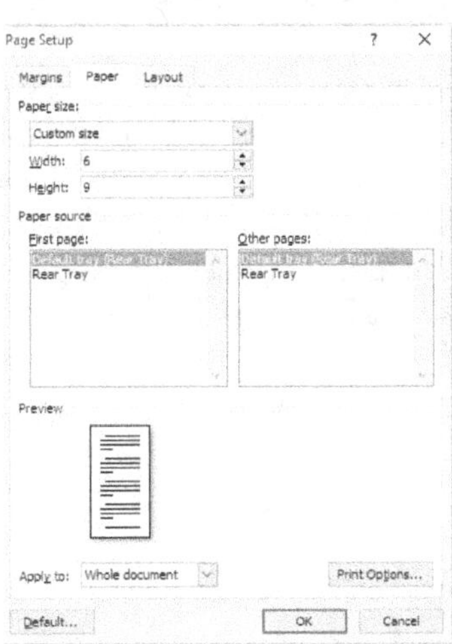

In the same page setup box, select the Margins tab. CreateSpace requires a minimum of .25 for the outside margins but recommend .5. I generally go with what is recommended so apply .5 to the top, bottom, and right margin. Leave the left margin with nothing in it because we are going to include that in the gutter margin. What you set your gutter margin to depends on the page count of your book.

24 to 150 pages requires the gutter margin to be set at .375
151 to 300 is .5
301 to 500 is .625
501 to 700 is .75
701 to 825 is .875

Type in your gutter margin, and next to Multiple Pages select Mirror Margins. Apply to Whole Document and click OK.

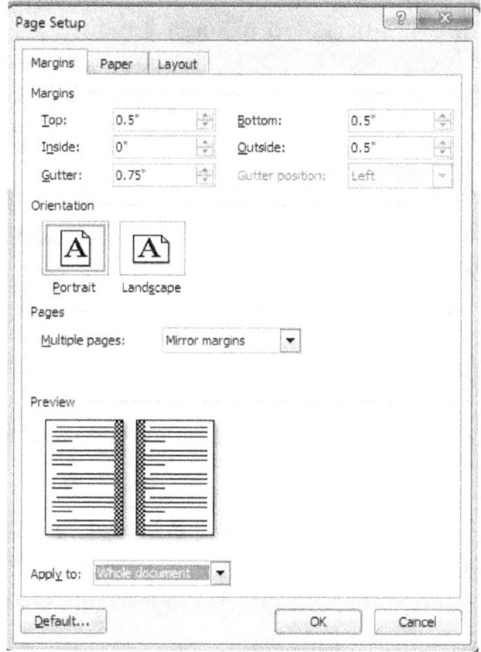

Finally to apply your paragraph indents, if you're having them. From the Page Layout tab, click on the arrow to the right of the Paragraph box. For my fiction I prefer indents between three and five spaces. Under Special select First Line, and under By enter your desired indent size, for example 0.5. Line spacing for printed books is generally single, so unless you really do want your book double spaced, select Single for Line Spacing. Finally in this box, decide on the space between paragraphs and type this by Spacing After. I generally use 10pt, but you might prefer a smaller size. Click OK. Save your document when you are happy with the way it looks.

Now you should be looking at your manuscript with two pages side by side rather than one at a time. When formatting your book for CreateSpace, the page you see in front of you on the right will actually be positioned on the left in the actual printed book. Chapter headings in paper books are always on the right, so go through your manuscript with that in mind. All chapter headings should be on the left side of the manuscript of your two page view. You might have to insert a few blank pages to get everything into position, but it is really worth the effort. Check your front and back matter with this fact in mind, and also insert blank pages where necessary to improve the look of the final result.

Save your finished manuscript, and then using the Save As option in the Microsoft emblem in the top left hand corner of your screen, save it again as a PDF file. This is what you will be loading on to CreateSpace.

Paper Cover

You can either create your cover online with CreateSpace's Cover Creator, or you can go to their site to calculate your book's spine with and download a template for it if you feel confident enough to design it yourself. The Cover Creator is really easy to use if you have your already designed cover for your Kindle book, and produces a nice finished product, although a beautiful and original spine can only be obtained by using the downloadable template. Cover images for CreateSpace must be a minimum of 300DPI, and that goes for any images that you have in the book also.

Publish on CreateSpace

If you haven't already, set up your CreateSpace account.

Start your new project, and from your member dashboard, select Add New Title. It's a simple process going through all the steps. I do suggest that you choose Guided as a Setup Process. If you don't want to purchase an ISBN, CreateSpace will assign one to your book for free.

Remember when choosing trim size and paper colour that you can't change this once it's been set. When you've loaded your cover and PDF manuscript up, you will get to review it with their online reviewer. Take this slowly, and go through each page. Download a review copy as well. You can then order your physical review proofs – as many as you like. Once you've received them and are happy with your paper book, log on to CreateSpace and approve it for sale and Distribution. You can actually approve it straight away, but that really is not a good idea, especially if this is your first published book.

Once that is done it will take a few days for it to appear beneath the Kindle version on Amazon, but it will be available for sale from CreateSpace themselves as well. Don't select publish on Kindle from the CreateSpace site, because this will have another Kindle version published based on the paper book. I did this, and a horrible distorted eBook hung around on Amazon for months, being bought by unsuspecting readers, and it was only when I started noticing bad reviews for formatting issues that I looked and found out what had happened. It's a much better idea to publish the Kindle book yourself.

One last little factoid here. Amazon keep a few copies of your printed book in stock because of their speedy delivery service. These books will go out first even though you have updated your CreateSpace book, so checking that your paper book looks really great in its actual physical form is a really good idea. If you do want to fix anything at a later point it’s a simple matter of loading up your corrected manuscript and following the same process.

MARKETING & THE PLATFORM

Marketing isn't about forcing or conning someone into buying something that they really don't want. At least it shouldn't be. It's about giving them the opportunity to want something that you have to sell. You have to provide something that will catch their interest enough to want your product. Often with books, the thing that interests brand new readers is the person behind the writing. You are the product so to speak. There is so much to read for free nowadays with millions of blogs and online articles out there, not to mention the millions of free eBooks floating around. You have to have something that will make paying actual cash for your book seem like a good investment. Give something of value or interest to be seen in the vast ocean of the online world.

Discoverability is also key. While your sales and marketing efforts are important, it's equally important for your books to be found in searches on Amazon. Your book has to be seen before anyone can purchase it. This is where your book's categories and tags also come into play. You want to be found by total strangers searching for a specific genre, topic, or word.

A lot of writers balk at the thought of trying to sell themselves or their books, but it is the only way to find new readers. It doesn't have to be hard selling though. In fact most people are put off by constantly being bombarded by sales pitches, and with self-published eBooks being so plentiful right now, advertisements for them are everywhere.

As you move further along your self-publishing path, you will eventually develop your own marketing plan, but it is important to have one. Before you publish your book you should draw up a list of what you're going to do to get it seen, which is why it is important to establish and maintain an online presence before you publish it. Start a blog, join Twitter, create a Facebook author page, join Google+, and sign up for any other sites you feel that you can manage such as LinkdIn, and Pinterest. You don't have to join all of them. You'll find that as time goes by and your sites grow that it will become quite time consuming to manage too many effectively.

Decide whether you're going to arrange for a book launch blog tour, and find out about free or paid for advertising for it. Get your author media kit ready. Paid advertising is something that sells books. Paid for reviews (other than from recognised places like Publisher's Weekly or Kirkus) on the other hand can get you into serious trouble with Amazon.

To advertise your books, look at Book Gorilla, People Reads, Betty Book Freak, The Daily Bookworm, BookBub, and Choosy Bookworm.

A Bit About the Platform

It's a good idea to consider the name you're going to use before setting up your online sites. Be very comfortable with the author name you decide to use. I say this from experience. I originally planned to publish my sci-fi/fantasy books under a totally different name to the one I use for my literary fiction, and actually did originally publish the first book in my series under that name. Not very much later I changed my mind and decided to use my own name. My books are very clearly what they are, and I absolutely respect my readers to know whether or not they want to read a genre that they don't like just because it's been written by me.

This is all very easy to change on Amazon, but not so much on sites around the internet that have already built up fans. For instance, once a page on Facebook has accumulated several hundred likes you can't change the name without asking Facebook for help. As anyone who has ever waited for return mail from Facebook will know – forget about it. I sent a couple of mails to them without reply, so now I maintain the page, having no intention of just disappearing one day and disrespecting those lovely people who actually have interest enough in what I have to say to have clicked that old like button. It can make for extra work and some confusion down the line though, so be very sure before you begin.

Must Love Blogs

Your blog is the flagship of your author platform. There are many sites where you can set up a free blog. My favourite is Wordpress. It's very user friendly and has a nice look and some very helpful features for Indie authors to make use of. At this point I make use of the free Wordpress.com site, but you do have the option of a paid for self-hosting site, which in the long run is the better choice. Wordpress.com allows scheduling of posts, so you can write posts in advance and load them up to go live later on. If you don't already have an active blog, and would like to get started then I suggest signing up with Wordpress. My largest piece of advice here comes to you not because I did it, but because I realised that I should have done it at the start at a point where I had too many followers to want to lose. This advice is simply to use your own author name as the name of your blog right from the start, which will also be in your blog's URL, and make for you to be found a lot easier in Google searches.

What and how often you post on your blog is up to you. My blog isn't only about books and writing, but about all aspects of my life and also pretty much anything I feel like sharing or chatting about. I love blogging and my blogging friends and community, so this is not a chore for me, but rather a pleasure. I don't only follow writer's blogs, but any that interest me, and I've found that this community above all is really vibrant and supportive. Blogging really will help you get your book news out there more than any other site in my opinion.

Website

Many Indies don't have a website, preferring to use their blog site instead, and this is fine. There are certain limits with the different blog sites. With a Wordpress.com free account, you can't sell paper books directly from your blog using PayPal, whereas you can from a website. You can make a stunning website, which will be good to use when you have promotions and new releases in the future, and want to run Rafflecopters and so on. Websites look professional, and are worthy tools in your Indie toolbox. You can create yours for free with Wix. Before you get started with this one I must tell you that once you have chosen your theme, colours, and fonts and actually published the site, you can't change that. You can change all of your content whenever you wish to afterwards, but your theme, colours, and fonts will stay the same so take your time deciding.

Facebook Page

Facebook isn't my playground at all to be honest, but I think it's important for authors to be visible in as many places as they can be. Apparently users of Pininterest are a whole lot more likely to click on a buy link than Facebook users, but it's good to have an author page there anyway. Some authors have different pages for each of their books, which is fine too if you have the time to keep up with all of them but I prefer just one page. If you write in completely different genres it could be easier for you to have a different page for each genre. If you absolutely detest Facebook so much that the very thought of signing up there makes you quiver with fear, then head over to Google+.

Google +

Google is a powerful force online, and you should make an effort to be present there. I like Google+ a whole lot more than Facebook. Full of friendly people and vibrant communities, I find it much easier to navigate than the ever changing book of faces with a lot less people hanging around looking for fights. As well as your own profile on G+ you can also set up a page if you like.

Circlescope is a handy app that shows you what's happening with your followers. Twitter has lots of people who will follow you, and then unfollow you later purely to boost their follower counts. This happens on G+ also, but with Circlescope it's easy to find them and unfollow them back. There is no point in following people who are not interacting with you.

Twitter

Some love it, some hate it, but for getting your news to possible hundreds of thousands of eyeballs in an instant it's pretty hard to beat. For the Indie author, Twitter is going to be one of your best marketing tools. One of the first things newly published Indies who are also new to Twitter do is to find and follow as many authors as they can. Nothing wrong with that, because Twitter Indies are super supportive. Do consider though that your potential readers are anyone out there at all, so don't follow authors to the exclusion of anyone else. Follow people who tweet about things that interest you other than writing. Fashion, gardening, rare varieties of eyelash mites – anything at all, and interact with them. Be genuine, and you'll cultivate friendships on all of your social networking sites. Not only is it really wonderful to make these new friends, you'll also find that mutual support with sharing and retweeting will find you even more new readers.

Who you follow back is up to you. I follow back pretty much anyone who follows me apart from obvious bots, pornography sites, and people who are following ten but have ten thousand followers. As I said, there is absolutely no point in following anyone who is not following you unless it's one of your idols, because if they're not following you, they can't see any of your tweets. What should you tweet? Certainly not only Buy My Book links. Twitter is another good place to actually enjoy yourself. Tweet photos, articles of interest, and share your blog posts there. Retweet others who retweet you, and pretty soon you'll have a wonderful flock of supportive Twitter friends. Use hashtags such as #amwriting or #amreading.

Images are always popular on Twitter. A nice way of posting your book links rather than just whacking the Amazon URL together with a tiny promotional tweet is to take a little time creating images with Picmonkey or your image editor of choice, where you type excerpts onto an appropriate picture. You can easily do this with inspiring quotes from books you've read other than your own also.

Twitter is also well known for those people who follow thousands, and then unfollow most of them later purely for the purpose of appearing to be really popular. Use the free Crowdfire app or JustUnfollow to find and unfollow them regularly or you will end up will piles of tweets in your feed from people who have no interest in what you have to say at all.

Joining the Goodreads Author Program is a good idea. How involved you get there is up to you, but it holds a massive amount of potential readers. It has been known to have hosted some spectacularly vicious barnies, but as with anywhere else these can be avoided by ignoring any attempts at hostility and not posting anything potentially inflammatory.

Sign up for Mailchimp, which is totally free until you hit the two thousand subscriber mark, at which point you will most definitely be able to afford their reasonable fees. It's very easy to use with their step by step tutorial. Sending out a newsletter, whether once a month or once every couple of months, is a great way to make sure that your readers don't forget about you, and where you can let them know about new books, freebies, or special offers. Put something that your particular audience will enjoy in every one, like a short story, a competition, a recipe, or information that you think will be of interest. This way they're more likely to look forward to your newsletters and open them rather than sending them to the trash.

The content you send in your newsletters must absolutely not be only about buying your book. Definitely announce your new books, but don't just send the same links ad nauseam. It's not hard to unsubscribe from a newsletter, nor is it hard to mark it as spam. You can however find ways to bring up your books in every newsletter by writing entertaining or useful articles about things to be found within their covers, and not published on your regular blog.

In closing this section, I must ask, have you heard about the "Oy, buy my book!" brigade? I'll be surprised if you haven't, because they truly are everywhere these days. Those self-published authors who post links to their books ten times a day on every site, page, and group that they can manage. They seldom have anything else to say, other than to promote their books. This is not good behaviour, and is unlikely to help your brand in any way.

Rotten Reviews and Terrible Trolls

You will get bad reviews. It's inevitable, I promise you. Take comfort in the fact that it's a rite of passage all writers go through. Every – single - one of them, and after the first one has you on the floor, bawling your eyes out, and inexplicably trying to chew your own foot off for a while, they're not so hard to deal with. Some are pretty funny, and some are just to be ignored. There are people out there who delight in trashing books, and sometimes the authors of books too, for reasons unknown to most decent humans. Sometimes it's jealousy, and sometimes it's just because they're mean. Sometimes also these one star stabs to the soul are perfectly legitimate in their author's hearts and minds, because they really didn't enjoy what you wrote for reasons that do or don't make sense to you. Whatever the reasons are for your one star clanger, you must never, ever, never, never, and I repeat, never respond to them. If you really need to share your pain then talk to a friend – preferably a writer friend, who will totally get you. I personally don't think that it's a good idea to respond to fabulous five star rave reviews either. "Liking" that wonderful review is good enough. The reviewer might actually not appreciate being gushed at by an unknown author, no matter how much you really want to catch a plane, find them, and kiss them on the lips. Reviews are for readers, good ones and bad ones. It's best for you to let them be.

Now the trolls on the other hand can be some crazy scary creatures. Try and avoid them at all costs, and be very wary of provoking any. After any amount of time cruising around our dear world wide web you're guaranteed to come across a couple. Whether it's something you'll read in a forum or on a blog or article that enrages you so badly you act before thinking, or a troll actually infiltrating your own sites for whatever reason, you need to throw away that pointy stick without poking that horrible hairy monster, turn around very quietly and run away. On other sites you're better off never getting involved with these people – ignore them, and they won't even know that you were there. On your own sites use your block, ban, and report buttons with gusto in the event of any sort of blow across your bows. I have a few times and that's been the end of that for me personally, but I have witnessed some pretty awful trollings online that were truly appalling to see, especially on Goodreads. Have no part in these things if you can help it.

When you do get a negative review, pass it on to that part of you who is the business – not the writer – figure out if there is anything to learn from it, in which case it becomes helpful, and if not, move right along and forget about it. Don't waste your valuable online time on trolls and hurtful reviews.

How much time of every day should you spend "marketing" online, versus how much time should you spend each day writing your next book? Writing your next book must always take priority. A couple of self-published books have gone on to be NYT bestsellers with break out first novels, but that's not the way this author life generally works. You have to produce more than one book. A little quirk that all of us readers have is the desire to read more from a writer we love. We'll read a book that we adore, and praise it from the rafters. We'll look for more books by the same author, and if there aren't any, we'll forget about it unless something pops up to remind us about it again. So schedule your daily writing time, and try and stick to it, doing other marketing and business related projects at other times of your day.

If you want to write books and earn a living from it, you are going to have to write and publish more books. If you're writing a series you probably won't see substantial sales until you have a couple of books out there. Don't panic about this though. Underlying anxiety fussing about getting this done could very well knobble your creativity and leave you staring at a blank computer screen. I read an article by Hugh Howey a long time ago, where he said that he didn't ever bother trying to market his first book until he'd published others. It was only his seventh book, Wool, that rocketed him to fame. I took his advice and I'm glad that I did. As you publish more, you learn so much more than you expect to after that bight eyed ecstasy when hitting the publish button for the very first time. Definitely do market and advertise your first book – of course you must, but don't let disappointing first sales put you off writing the next or let marketing consume all of your time. You need time to build a readership. Patience and tenacity are what the Indie needs to succeed.

Pirates Ahoy!

Before you actually publish your first book for purchase you might be over the moon at the fact that anyone wants to read it badly enough to steal it. Many really successful Indies stand by this credo, and many also don't. I've had my books pirated on too many sites to count now. Many of these sites will zap you with malware if you try to download a book, but many of them really do download free copies of your books to whoever clicks the button. Your choices of action are to either ignore them or issue take down notices. It is true that the people who download stolen books are highly unlikely to search for and buy your book. They'll simply steal another one. Piracy is a terrible scourge though, so the more take down notices we send, the better.

Paying the Bills

Will you earn a living? Probably not to begin with. Not many books have shot to stardom without the work being put in. I can't begin to explain or understand how anyone would decide to write purely for the purpose of making money if they don't love the writing process. I believe firmly that writing – good and meaningful writing – can come only from a writer who is writing for the story, and not for the money. The vast majority of authors don't actually make a lot of money, but many of them do earn enough to live a comfortable if modest life. Possibly anyone with the technical ability to write can make loads of cash writing perfect text books, but fiction comes from the passionate calling of someone who has to write as much as they have to breathe. I don't approve of get rich quick schemes by internet marketers to churn out dozens and dozens of cons pretending to be books.

I do, however, believe that we who do write because it is our love deserve to sell our books. The point of writing these books is to give something to anyone who reads them. We want to impart something to the reader, and not merely to relieve them of their cash, and this is the way it should be. I strongly feel that if we believe in our books, we should never be afraid to put them out there for sale, and when we do put them out there, we should do that part of the job to the very best of our abilities, gathering as much knowledge about what we need to do as possible.

Believing in your work and yourself is a vital part of selling your books. If you have an underlying belief that your book really isn't good enough, and can only be sold by tricking people into buying it, trust me, you won't sell many books. There's something to be said for having a sound and planned marketing strategy for the books you wrote with love – they deserve to find eyes that love them.

If you have a day job that pays your bills while you build your backlist on your way to writing full time, that's fine, although you won't have as much time as you'd like to write. Consider creating other income streams apart from your fiction. Well written and researched non-fiction can be such an income stream. There are always people searching for information or help, and you could very well be the one to assist them. Consider things that you're good at. Things that you know about. These could be hobbies or interests, and also personal or medical challenges that you've overcome. Writing non-fiction can help pay your bills while you write the fiction books that you love.

There are also many other places online where you can boost your income. Websites that will pay for your short stories or articles, as well as places such as Zazzle, where you can sell artwork or designs on all sorts of things from mugs to t-shirts. You don't actually have to be overly artistic to do this either. Catchy, clever quotes in nice fonts could do just as well.

But is it a Job?

Many writers feel guilty about the time they spend writing. Sometimes it's their guilty secret, and not sharing what they're doing means that they can only write when nobody is watching. Often, the people in their lives add fuel to this mindset, implying or sometimes saying outright, that writing is a bit of self-indulgent fluff. Get a "proper" job is a favourite. When you're starting out and earning a few measly dollars a month, this sentiment seems valid. If writing is your passion, you'll probably "steal" hours from your days or weeks of "real life" to do it, but it's unlikely that you'll ever really know if writing could ever be your life's work this way. Don't let this happen if you know that this is what you're meant to be doing. Even if you still are at the point where you can't justify full time writing without starvation and penury, and you can only claim two hours writing time a day, claim those hours forcefully and emphatically. You are a writer. Say so, and firmly squash any attempts at belittling your chosen work. Of course it's a job. Whoever started the notion that you shouldn't get pleasure from your work, and then still carry on doing that for the rest of your life has a lot to answer for.

Few are called to write, and even fewer embrace that calling. It's no easier than working nine to five at any other profession – sometimes it can be much, much harder. Just like any work, you must show up every day. You must create totally new sentences. You must draw on the unreal, and make it real. Do yourself the honour of respecting your amazing gift enough to put in the hours, and the work it will take to make it real. Success rarely comes in the form of a lottery win. Success always requires real work. So yes – it most certainly is a job. Instant success for authors is magical thinking, and best ignored when thought of or brought up by an unthinking loved one. If you want to make self-publishing and selling your writing your full time work, then you're going to have to step up to the plate, and do everything that needs to be done to make that possible, including all the non-creative nuts and bolts things along the way. The only way to do this properly is to tackle the entire process as you would any other job that you would show up for every day to earn a wage.

Not only is it a job, it's your own business. How much more important is that? You are a publisher. How you see it is entirely up to you though. I've embraced the concept of the Absolute Indie, so yes, this is my job. In an ideal world we would all be able to support ourselves while doing the work that we love. Life doesn't work like that unfortunately, and instead many people go to jobs every day that they really don't love only because they have to pay their bills. Many bestselling authors started out by writing in any minute they had to spare, but still keeping their day jobs for years, and this is what many intrepid writers are doing right now. Those fortunate enough to have all their time to dedicate to their writing can approach it in any way they choose. Some see writing as something that only happens when they're inspired, or when the "muse" comes to sit on their shoulder and whisper into their ear. There are others at the other end of the spectrum who feel driven to force themselves to write and churn out as much as they possibly can. I prefer to hit a happy medium.

I'm the CEO of my business, and most of the employees in it as well. While writing is my first love, I also take my publishing journey very seriously, and do all that I do as my job. I have set working hours which I try to stick to, and times to tackle the various aspects of it. Obviously this doesn't always work out, life being what it is, but I no longer beat myself up when I don't get something done in the time I've set for it. The further along the Indie road you travel the busier it gets, so a little compassion is sometimes required when a self-imposed deadline is missed. My kind of operation won't be for everyone, but some may like it. I find that without my schedule I spend more time on my favourite tasks and eventually the ones that aren't at the top of my happy list pile up to the point where I have to spend so much time catching up that I only dislike them more.

I insist on writing every day because I choose to do so. I believe in what I'm doing with my writing, and so writing takes precedence over anything else that isn't important, like making sure the family don't have to beg for crusts from the neighbours and that sort of thing. When it's my time to write, the housework can wait, the coffee shop get together with buddies can wait, the – you get the picture. The fact that I'm not really in the mood to write on any particular day never, ever takes precedence over the bigger picture. Unless there's a real emergency that needs attending to, I write during my hours allocated for writing, with everything else switched off. If you choose to watch television rather than write, then that's your personal choice, but if you truly believe in yourself as a writer, then you have to make yourself some rules, and stick to them no matter what anyone else says or believes about your choice of career.

Time management can seem a little daunting to the creative soul, but things like cooking larger meals and freezing portions to defrost later, and realising that maybe you having to shine all the windows every Tuesday might not have to be a real thing can help. Make sure your family realise how serious you are about your working hours, and delegate firmly. Your writing isn't a hobby so demand respect for it when not freely given.

Just because you're your own boss doesn't mean you have to be a limp-wristed boss and give yourself all sorts of leeway. Plan your book from outline to publication, and have a (realistic) deadline to meet for that publication date even if the only person who knows it is you, and even if you miss it, you'll have made every effort to meet it and will have learned something for the next book deadline you set yourself. You'll be amazed at how quickly good habits are formed, and you'll get to the point where if life keeps you away from your writing time and your work, you'll be very uncomfortable with that.

Writing is your passion and your love, and when you're writing you don't have to think about budgets, income, marketing, book creation or any other thing other than the lonely cry of your dragon as she tumbles down to the surface of her world with broken wings, but if you want to make writing your business as well as your pleasure it will be best if you set it up as such. I'm not sure why, but when I set myself up as a business rather than as only a writer, I found that my writing hours became so much more productive. The time I spend working on the "business" of being The Absolute Indie seems to make the working hours allocated to writing a lot less prone to blockages and distractions, and my creativity is in no way hampered.

Once you've decided on the path of an Indie, and are set to devote yourself fulltime to this end, it's time to carve out your game plan. Setting a fixed time in every day for your writing is your first job. This is time when nothing gets to intrude on you and your creation. This is the time for as many unicorns and as much elf dust as your artistic soul requires. When you move on to the business hours of your days, the unicorns must head over the ridge to play, and you must concentrate on what needs to be done for you to move further along in your profession. Don't fall into the belief that lucre is a filthy word, and that selling your art is dirty. Just because it can contain beauty, inspiration, joy, and laughter doesn't make a book any less of a commodity than a movie. When you're not in the process of creating that beauty from that very special place that only writers have within, then you must be busy with the business of getting it into the hands of the people who will be moved by it to inspiration, joy, knowledge or laughter. It's not a sin for a writer to work on packaging and product and selling. In this new world of publishing it's essential – part of the job. If your aim is to have your books read, then you're going to have to toss the thought that artists can't do anything other than create art. That's totally not true, unless you want it to be. Getting paid for your work is your goal and your validation. It's a craft. A craft is work. Craftsmen get paid. So let's get to the job.

ON BEING THE ABSOLUTE INDIE

What are your goals? We start any project in life with a vision of what we hope to see on its completion. Without goals life doesn't have any particular purpose, and we simply cruise along, moving with the tides and eddies of external forces. Sometimes our goals are vague. We want enough to eat, a nice home, and happy children. Sometimes they're a little more specific such as we want to write a book. An epic love story maybe, or a fantasy to sit alongside Lord of the Rings. This is where goal setting comes in to play if we want to achieve our goal. Write down where you want your writing career to be in five years, and make that your vision and your goal. Believe in yourself and work towards that vision every day.

The Job Description

Your first tool is determination. You know that feeling when you put off exercising? Could be just a tiny bit of guilt or a large chunk of self-loathing. That feeling when you put off writing seems just the same to me. That feeling when you're staring at your computer screen, and rather than fingers flying over your keyboard, all you can concentrate on is the sinking feeling of failure – that dull little ache in your centre, reminding you that you can't do it. You have sixty thousand words to write before you'll even know if you really can write a decent story. It could turn out to be absolute trash. It could bomb so badly that the reverberations of your shame will be felt around the globe. Your time would be much better spent doing something you really can do, like dusting your collection of cute miniature frogs. Well. The Absolute Indie leaves those gorgeous little porcelain amphibians nestling in their powdery coatings for another day, and ploughs ahead no matter how hard it seems. Don't give up so quickly. Use your entire allocated writing time to write. Write a paragraph about anything at all, and see where it takes you. Grab a Post-It note and write SO WHAT? in big red letters, stick it on the corner of your monitor, and start writing.

Write whatever comes – eventually you'll hit your stride, and you can delete the bad stuff when you're done. Do whatever you have to do to get your tale down in words. So what if it bombs? You'll never know if you have a bestseller until it's written and out there for all to see. If it bombs, you'll crawl out of the steaming crater, snorting ash from your nostrils, and carry on writing, having learned what a book needs to bomb, so you'll know what not to do next time. Stomp on the doubt and fear, and evict all those intruding thoughts of frog dusting, and write anyway. Latch on to that inner place that knows the joy of putting words out there, and write every day. Even if the words you write seem like utter drivel, you'll eventually then get to experience that other feeling – the one where you grin and picture your leather-clad, pipe-wielding muse laughing with wild joy, as she grinds the heel of her stiletto into the unconscious cranium of that devil called Doubt. Nothing beats the ecstasy of accomplishment.

Just the fact that you have that unbearable ache to write a book in the first place makes you awesome. Believe in your calling, write through all the fear, and keep your eye on the prize. The fear is always there in all of life's journeys when there's epic work to be done, and always to be conquered, because there really never is any going around it, no matter how many books you get to write. So writing is the first and most important job of any in the day. Five hundred words or five thousand words is an equal accomplishment in my view. Don't let your eye be constantly drawn to the word count, and never beat yourself up if you only manage three legible sentences. Writing every day is your goal, but nobody can ever truly say that it's always going to be easy.

Your aim is to write, publish, and sell your work. Sounds simple enough, but there are many different things to be done along the way, and if you break down your days specifically to do these tasks, you could very well find that when your writing time comes around you don't have those "I don't know what to write" moments very often. There's comfort in order, even for creatives, and when you're not stressed the writing should flow right out. From inception to completion, here's the core of what you need to be doing, when you're doing it all.

Brainstorming is a huge part of the job. Not only thinking of ideas for future books, but also new and interesting ways to get those books to readers. Find out about the tried and tested ways that successful authors sell their books, but also take some specific time to look for less well trodden marketing paths. Look at how other commodities get to their buyers, and see if other methods can be used to sell books.

Researching your facts is another important part of the job. Readers will be offended if you insult their intelligence or common sense with blatantly incorrect statements, unless you're attempting to do so on purpose in obviously silly ways that are meant to bring on a chuckle. Even if you're writing fantasy or science fiction, your story about unicorns and fairies or the invasion of the planet Urg, you have to make sure that your reader's sense of possibility isn't stretched too far to become immersed in the tale. These days with the internet, finding out facts is easy. If you want your story to be set in Paris, and you've never been there, you can use Google Earth Street View for your settings for instance, so this makes this part of the job more fun than work.

Reading, believe it or not, has been you researching your craft for all of your life. Writers of fiction aren't people who don't like to read. Those non-reading few who really do make the lists are generally celebrities or people who have had some serious stuff go down in their lives, and they share these tales with the help of ghost writers. Reading is a part of your job, and not something to find time for. Allocate time for regular reading and don't be guilty about enjoying it. Reading bad writing sometimes is not a bad thing either, because it shows you how not to write.

Writing is the same as any craft. While you may have a natural inborn talent and love for it, you're only going to learn it by learning from those already doing it well. All of those times when you were lost in the snowy magic of Narnia, or lost in the love of two paper people to the point where you had no idea that the people in the coffee shop were staring at the warm, fat tears flowing down your cheeks, your little black box was learning. Your mind was taking in the syntax and the grammar; taking note of verbs and adverbs – aaargh adverbs! Actually, I like a good, well placed adverb or two, so—.

The Absolute Indie is a very busy bunny, and I can say from personal experience that if you're on this road for real, it can become difficult to find time for the other things you love to do. Don't ever lose reading as you struggle to choose what you have "spare" time for. Reading is as vital as writing itself. In this wild explosion of self-publishing, don't be too picky. Make your reading list a fifty-fifty list – half of all your old traditionally published rock stars, and the other half Indie writers. There are appalling stories written by both sides of the spectrum, and I find that if I read one after the other in non-ending sequence I retain my equilibrium. Traditional, Indie, and so on.

If you plan on publishing children's or picture books, the illustrating or taking photos would slot into your weekly work schedule.

Proofreading and editing of their writing are daily chores for some authors (not this one anymore). Many authors like to meticulously go over what they've produced on any given day, and that's fine. I prefer to wait till the book is finished.

Outsourcing for various services will fall in the job description at some point, unless you really want to do everything for every book yourself. It's nice to know where to find needed services when they're required, so I keep a file with names, contact details, and services offered on hand, and add to it whenever I come across an artist or proofreader that I'm impressed with. Also keep files for any work that you do have done for you with receipts or model releases if they were required.

Creating covers will be part of the job, whether it's designing them yourself or putting together your vision for them for a hired designer. I have my book cover ready to publish before I finish whichever book I'm working on at the time.
Formatting and publishing aren't weekly jobs, unless you write very short books or are incredibly prolific, but they can be very time-consuming and stress-inducing when they do come around. Keep a file with all you need to know about the processes for both your Kindle and paper book formatting for easy future reference, rather than trying to rely on your memory.

Marketing and market research are a big part of your job. Probably not so much just after your first published book though. That's the time you should be zooming along writing and publishing your second. Once you are ready to stick your toe into the world of marketing, it's a good idea to go in with a plan. I wish I'd known this when I first found out that marketing was something I'd have to do myself. The core of your marketing will be on the social networks, and planning your strategies in advance will make your life much easier as you grow.

You need a presence on social networking sites, with a blog being the most important. You get to choose how many sites to join and how much of your time you spend on them. It's very easy to have hours go by while chatting on Facebook and checking your Twitter feed, which can lead to days where no writing gets done, and that's bad, so scheduling your online time is the way to go. When I first joined my own networking sites it was easy to visit each and every one of them every day, but as they grew this became impossible. When you are writing out your plan for your workdays, think individual site when you allocate marketing times, rather than all of them every day.

Advertising and promotion can either be paid or free, but it is a very important part of your business, so definitely have a file for this. The best free promotion you can get is word of mouth and visibility for yourself or your books on other bloggers sites. Book blog tours are a great way to find new readers for when you launch your babies or have a promotion. Paid advertising is something that you should do if you can afford it. Many of the paid advertising services that I've listed in this book also offer free listings for when your books are offered at a discount or for free, and their newsletter recipients are always growing. Keep a file of all the ones you like, and keep ongoing records of how your books sold when using them for future reference.

Budgeting and accounting might seem a little silly when you're writing your first book, but down the line you'll find the facts and figures interesting to say the least, or useful whether your books sell loads or just a few. If you do have a budget set aside for work to be done getting your book to publication point, and for buying paper copies to sell yourself, keep records of all your expenditure and sales, so you'll know when you start making a profit and also if there's anything you could do better next time around.

Creating income streams other than writing are worth thinking about, so schedule time for that it it's something you want to work on. Writers generally start out not even considering doing anything other than writing, but as they grow and learn along their self-publishing journeys they develop and hone some very particular skill along the way. They can offer their own services in their fields of experience then, such as proofreading or cover design, or whatever it is that they're good at. You're extremely unlikely to make much money from selling your books when you begin your Indie trip, so utilise any other talents you may have to help with cash if you aren't in a situation where you're already financially comfortable.

I've seen a few comments by Indie authors saying that they don't ever read Indie books because they've had some bad experiences with them previously. This really is exactly like punching yourself in the face. As an Indie author you must read books by others in your field. It's also a good idea to review and promote other Indie authors, not only because this is for the good of the whole tribe, and Indies are the most supportive bunch around, but also every one you read will help you in honing your craft. It can't be denied that there are some proper stinkers out there, but there are also some truly great pieces of literature written by self-published authors. The bad ones will show you how not to write, and the beauties can only inspire you.

A small thought on writing peer reviews here. If you are an actual book reviewer, feel free to have at it with well deserved one star scathing reviews wherever you'd like to place them. This is your right as a reader. If you are also a published author, think a little before you do this. Even if the negative review is fair and true, you could still become the target of revenge attacks on your own books. This has happened to authors over and over on both Amazon and Goodreads, and it surprises me that it still is happening. You don't have to post a glowing review for an awful book. You don't have to post a review at all for it if you hate it. I personally have never posted a negative review anywhere. I simply close the eyeball offender and forget about it. There will be more than enough readers, who are not also authors, who will do the necessary as far as reviews go, so if possible, try and avoid your books or yourself being trolled.

Hours of Business

I've often gotten out of bed, and apart from making sure that everyone is fed and watered, sat in front of my computer for the whole day and into the night when I've been on an epic writing roll or had a deadline to meet. Occasionally this is a fabulous adventure, but not really very healthy as a way to go about things for any length of time. If your official working day is set to begin at nine in the morning you can bath and dress and sit down to a nice breakfast without any stress. If you write down all you have to do in your home and life on a daily basis, you can prepare your schedule from there. Lists can be your friends. Find the hours you need to do your work, write them down, and do your best to stick to them, and you'll eventually find that this actually makes your life easier rather than giving you more work. There's great joy to be had when you hold up the end result of your discipline. So plan your writing life. Allocate the time that you will write every day. Stick to it. Write whether you feel like it or not during your allocated writing time. Stephen King has done this all his life, and just look where it got him.

Annual Vacation

This coming year is the first since the beginning of my self-publishing journey that I'm contemplating taking an official holiday. Not a holiday from writing – I couldn't do that if I tried, and I wouldn't want to, because writing is my love as well as my work. A holiday from the nuts and bolts work once a year is probably something that many Indie authors forego, especially in the beginning of their careers. Always rushing to meet the next deadline or goal can leave you really frazzled, and not at all keen to open up your email in the mornings, because you know that there will be so many notifications. Marketing yourself involves a lot of interaction on social media, and as your online connections grow you one day find yourself in the position that even if you only did that all day, you still wouldn't be able to respond to everything. This causes a lot of stress, so the thought of not trying to keep up for even a single day doesn't occur.

I'm sure that many of the Indie authors I've seen to simply disappear forever at some point for no given reason, after years of being busy, busy, busy around and about the internet every day probably reached implosion point, and rather than keep trying to accomplish the impossible, gave up entirely. The thing with your online tribe is that their expectations of you are a lot lower than what you may think they are. They don't want you to run around like a loon, making yourself ill rather than let a comment or blog post go unanswered for more than ten minutes. They're often just as busy or even busier than you are, and the fact that they are your tribe means that they like you, so they will understand if you take a little time off.

Whether it's a couple of weeks, or even one week, during your official leave period only save up the most important notifications to deal with when you're back to work, and most definitely delete all other notifications. Start fresh, relaxed and invigorated.

Tools of the Trade

You are the chief tool. Your talent and your need to put pen to paper and make stuff up are what have made you that most magical of creatures, often found starving in garrets through time all over the world, busily working at the craft that won't be denied an outlet. Try not to go for the starving in a garret thing if you can help it, but if you can't and you still must write, then put your business cap on and start thinking like a boss so that even if you have to work at jobs you hate to pay the rent, you have a vision and a map set out for where you want to go. Once you have a nice list of books with sales ticking over you can lose the crappy jobs and stick to what you love. In today's world you're extremely unlikely to be able to support yourself or your family on the back of your first, or second book, but if you diligently keep them coming, you stand a good chance of doing just that down the road a bit.

We know that all the old classics were written with pen and paper or on those fabulous old clacking typewriters, but these days pretty much everyone has a computer of some kind. You know where you're most comfortable writing, but the ideal for any writer is to have an office – a room of their own that is off limits except by invitation to anyone else. A comfortable chair and a desk or table to hold your computer equipment, your collection of three hundred and fifty two gel pens (ahem), drawers or cabinets for your stationery, reference materials and files. While ideal, it isn't always possible to have your own office, and if not, try your best to at least claim a corner where you will not be disturbed or have your "stuff" touched or otherwise interfered with.

Obviously you must have a connection to the internet, or access to it from your laptop somewhere, preferably daily, where you can keep up to date with online business and social networking. Social networking sites are right up there with the most important tools of your trade to spread the word of your books and find new readers.

Reference material these days is so freely and immediately available online so we don't need loads of space to store things, and most of our paperwork is stored on our computers. It's still good to have a place for a few files to keep what we do need in paper form safely stored. Writing, publishing, and selling our books is our business, so we need to keep records of what we're spending and how much we're earning. Contracts, tax information, and other documents need to be printed out also.

If you don't use a diary now, you'll find that as your publishing life grows you'll need one if you're going to remember everything. Get a proper diary, and don't rely on scraps of paper. My diaries have saved my bacon on more than one occasion when I've had to refer back to something. I write everything in them, from publication dates to daily To Do lists.

Keep your author media kit up to date. Open a folder especially for this on your computer and put your bio of around two hundred to two hundred and fifty words, your author photo, all of the links to all of your sites as well as global links to your books. If you already have a published book, have a copy of the book cover and blurb. If you are soon to publish, have the same, as well as excerpts from any editorial reviews you may already have. This will make quick work of sending this information when you are invited to guest blog or go on a book launch tour or cover reveal. It is also good to have all of this information on a static page on your blog and website, so that any book reviewers can simply get all the information about you that they need. Rather than have different links posted for each of your books on all of Amazon's sites around the world, get yourself global links which automatically takes anyone who clicks on them to the country that they're in.

What Next?

If you get it all right straight out the gates I'll be— surprised. But very happy for your miracle. As with any job, The Absolute Indie will probably make mistakes along the way, and that's alright too. We always keep our eyes on the prize, fix our stumbles, and know better next time, because what's next is your brand new shiny next manuscript. All formatted and ready to go, just waiting for all that wonderful stuff from your scribbler's heart to transfer itself to the published page. Finish each of your books, and move right on to the next. Not every book can be hugely successful, in fact very few are, so never be disheartened so much if a book doesn't do fabulously that you stop writing. All the greats had many failures on their paths to the readers who finally loved them.

Updating Your Published Books

It's good practice to have clickable links of all your published books in the front matter of all of them, so every time you publish a new one, you should go and update your backlist. Also, if you write non-fiction books and any information in them changes with time, then definitely make sure to update so they stay current and useful for their purpose. This is as simple as reloading your updated manuscripts. When a typo magically appears in your already published book, you can fix it, reload it, and even change your cover if you fancy. The new book file you load for your eBook gets updated quickly, but it will take up to seventy two hours for your cover update, so don't worry if they don't happen at the same time. Make sure to keep copies of all your latest manuscripts as word documents in files, just in case.

Beware of one thing though. If you update your currently published book you will lose nothing. All your reviews, good and bad, will remain. All your ranking history will remain also. If you unpublish your book and then republish your revised version, you're sending it out as a newbie again. This is recommended in some cases

where a book gets absolutely trashed in the review section for some reason, and generally needs major work to get it back to where your vision for it is.
But if you have more good reviews than bad ones, rather sit and consider for a while. You can easily fix all the mistakes you've made in your bright eyed eager first rush to publish. Write in capitals right at the beginning of your book blurb – This Version Re-edited and Updated on Date if you like. Or reformatted as the case may be. If your book is still brand new with only ten one star stinkers, unpublish it with haste. Then give it a proper makeover and publish it as a totally new book. Otherwise consider what you could lose.

Remember that all books get bad reviews. If every reader across the globe all liked the same book then we'd only need one. I get immediately suspicious of books with only five star reviews when there are more than twenty of them. Very occasionally is a book this superb to every single eyeball – there are some, but they are the exception rather than the rule. There are many unscrupulous people out there who will charge you to write glowing reviews of your book without ever having read it, and unfortunately many unscrupulous "writers" who will pay them to do so. Don't ever do this dear scribbler. The Absolute Indie loves and believes in the words of his soul. If you truly think that your writing is rubbish enough that you have to purchase praise, then—. Need I say more?

The final point on this subject is the possibility of inserting yourself fully up some future readers nostrils who have bought your original book, and now purchase this one later not realising it's the same thing. You have three days to return an eBook to Amazon for a full refund, but if you don't check it out in those days you have to keep it. (P.S. Amazon : Three days is WAAAY too long for this!) I always make a point of checking the books I buy fairly quickly, but this is only because I very almost made a very expensive Terry Pratchett double buy, so if you've had a lot of sales and the changes you made to your book are major, it might be worthwhile keeping it up and asking Amazon to send out a notification that it's been completely updated instead.

Unless you've paid for everything for your book to be put together by experienced professionals, I'm pretty sure that at some point you're going to be experienced enough yourself to know that it could be better. Once you have a couple of books published you might want to change their packaging so that your "brand" is recognisable. If you have a series, as it grows, your vision for the covers might change, and the process of going about doing this is going to be a lot of fun. The fact that you're changing and updating means that any reader who has already purchased your books is going to get the "Instant Order Update" from Amazon, so there is no risk of double buy rage coming your way, and with a bit of luck the new packaging will entice many new readers. The old version of your eBook stays live on the site for sale until the new version appears. Your paper book will be unavailable for purchase during the review time, so do this at a time when you're not actively promoting. Reviews generally take twelve hours. As I said before, paper books already in stock will be sold before any updated ones come in.

Publishing on Smashwords and Other Platforms

At this point in time I'm an Amazon only author, so this section isn't going to be long. The Absolute Indie, however, chooses where and when they publish their books. You totally own your business. I always reserve the right to change my mind in the future as far as to where I sell my books. One of my stories has been published by a publisher so if anyone fancies picking a nit this makes me a hybrid publisher – Indie and traditionally published. This book is all about publishing on Amazon, but in case you do decide to publish elsewhere as well I suggest that you download Mark Coker's free book available on Amazon, the Smashwords Style Guide, on how to go about loading your book on to Smashwords, and follow the steps carefully to meet the meatgrinder's demands. To make sure that your book is distributed to Barnes & Noble, iTunes, and so on you must get their formatting process spot on. Two tips to take specific note of are that you must have the words Smashwords Edition in your front matter, and also the meatgrinder absolutely hates empty space anywhere. Use your Show/Hide feature to find and remove any extra carriage returns. As I've said earlier, consider this carefully as a newly published author. My personal experience has been that the sales on these other channels don't justify the loss of the KDP Select perks when you're just starting out, and because having your books removed from these other outlets at a later date really is a bit of a nightmare. I recommend that you make use of KDP Select for the first three month period before you make the decision, and if you do then decide to go this route be sure to remove your book from KDP, and wait until the very last day of the enrolment period is over before loading your book anywhere else.

And So We Part For Now

I wish you well dear Indie writer. I admire your courage. The courage it took or will yet take to write your book to the end, and the courage to lay that book before the world. Remember always to admire yourself also. This road is hard, and not for the faint-hearted, but it really can be the way to great fulfilment if you choose to make it so. May the road before you be filled with the joy of letting loose your fabulous talent, and more joy as you settle in to fulfilling your life's purpose. Here's to learning and growing, and hopefully not too many little falls along the way. We are all together on this path, to cheer each other on, to celebrate each other's successes as well as our own, and to help along the way whenever we can. Be kind when one of your tribe may stumble and fall, and help them up rather than enjoying the show. Many will help you too. There are books of mine out there in the world that I dearly wish I could make disappear – those rookie books, gleefully sent out into the ether – that may or may not come back to haunt me some day, but overall I regret not one single second of my crazy trip to becoming The Absolute Indie. I appreciate all my falls now, because they made me learn what I needed to know about my trade, as you must learn too. I hope that this book has helped you to avoid all those things that now make me blush. If it has, then all the falls have been worthwhile. This is only the beginning of the world of the Indie writer. Don't believe for a second that the time to succeed as a self-published author is past. It will morph and change, and the sooner you finish and publish your book, the sooner you get to be a part of it. Start your journey right now, and be the very best that you can be. The Absolute Indie.

Book Notes

Title

Genre

Premise & Plot - Outline

Settings

Characters

NAME
APPEARANCE

CHARACTERSTICS

STORYLINE FOR THIS CHARACTER

NAME
APPEARANCE

CHARACTERSTICS

STORYLINE FOR THIS CHARACTER

NAME

APPEARANCE

CHARACTERSTICS

STORYLINE FOR THIS CHARACTER

NAME

APPEARANCE

CHARACTERSTICS

STORYLINE FOR THIS CHARACTER

NAME

APPEARANCE

CHARACTERSTICS

STORYLINE FOR THIS CHARACTER

NAME

APPEARANCE

CHARACTERSTICS

STORYLINE FOR THIS CHARACTER

NAME

APPEARANCE

CHARACTERSTICS

STORYLINE FOR THIS CHARACTER

NAME

APPEARANCE

CHARACTERSTICS

STORYLINE FOR THIS CHARACTER

Secondary Characters

Research

Research Notes

Wordcount

Monday					
Tuesday					
Wednesday					
Thursday					
Friday					
Saturday					
Sunday					

Monday					
Tuesday					
Wednesday					
Thursday					
Friday					
Saturday					
Sunday					

Monday					
Tuesday					
Wednesday					
Thursday					
Friday					
Saturday					
Sunday					

Monday					
Tuesday					
Wednesday					
Thursday					
Friday					
Saturday					
Sunday					

Monday					
Tuesday					
Wednesday					
Thursday					
Friday					
Saturday					
Sunday					

Monday					
Tuesday					
Wednesday					
Thursday					
Friday					
Saturday					
Sunday					

Monday					
Tuesday					
Wednesday					
Thursday					
Friday					
Saturday					
Sunday					

Monday					
Tuesday					
Wednesday					
Thursday					
Friday					
Saturday					
Sunday					

Monday					
Tuesday					
Wednesday					
Thursday					
Friday					
Saturday					
Sunday					

Monday					
Tuesday					
Wednesday					
Thursday					
Friday					
Saturday					
Sunday					

GOALS

What are your writing goals? Do you want to make a living writing books? Are you writing a series? How many books do you want to publish per year. List your hopes and expectations here. The book you're writing now, and also the possible titles and blurbs of future novels or non-fiction works. Set realistic goals, so as not to set yourself up for self-recrimination. As with all aspects of life, it's important not to be too harsh on yourself, while at the same time not being too soft either. So—what is your intention for yourself for this year and beyond? Set only goals which mirror that intention, and work only toward that end.

Editing Notes & Reminders

Editing Notes & Reminders

Services Page (proofreader, editor, cover designer, formatter, illustrator, etc)

Name: ______________________________
Email address: ______________________________
Phone: ______________________________
Service: ______________________________
Date Reserved: ______________________________
Deadline: ______________________________
Cost: ______________________________
Notes: ____
____

Name: ______________________________
Email address: ______________________________
Phone: ______________________________
Service: ______________________________
Date Reserved: ______________________________
Deadline: ______________________________
Cost: ______________________________
Notes: ____
____

Name: ______________________________
Email address: ______________________________
Phone: ______________________________
Service: ______________________________
Date Reserved: ______________________________
Deadline: ______________________________
Cost: ______________________________
Notes: ____
____

Name: ______________________________
Email address: ______________________________
Phone: ______________________________
Service: ______________________________
Date Reserved: ______________________________
Deadline: ______________________________
Cost: ______________________________
Notes: ____
____

Formatting To Do List

Make new folders for master manuscripts

CreateSpace :______________________________
Amazon Kindle :______________________________
ePub :______________________________
Smashwords :______________________________
:______________________________
:______________________________

Format for Kindle

Use Show/Hide ¶ to check for hidden unwanted formatting such as Tab use, and remove

Insert book's front matter

Set Indents and Spacing – Settings for this book

Alignment :______________________________
Indentation :______________________________
Spacing :______________________________

Check that there are page breaks before each chapter :______________________________

Fonts used for this book :______________________________

Check that all clickable links work :______________________________

Add author bio and previews of other books to back matter

Create Table of Contents

Go to page selected for table of contents.

____

Type the words Table of Contents.

____

Type out chapter heading names or numbers.

____

Bookmark each chapter heading.

Highlight chapter heading.

From INSERT menu select BOOKMARK.

Type in bookmark name without spaces.

Click ADD.

Return to typed table of contents, and insert a bookmark called toc.

From the typed table of contents highlight each chapter heading, right click and HYPERLINK to associated bookmark from Place in this book. Repeat for all.

Go to each chapter heading in the book and link back to your toc bookmark.

Remove hidden bookmarks.

Hyperlink Notes:

Converting with Calibre

***** FIRST SAVE FORMATTED MANUSCRIPT AND MAKE A COPY

Save As
Other Formats
Select WEB PAGE, FILTERED
Save

Open Calibre
Select ADD BOOKS
Select CONVERT BOOKS
Select OUTPUT FORMAT as ePub
Fill in book's title and your author name
From Table of Contents tab select Force Table of Contents
Click OK

Open Kindle Previewer
Select OPEN BOOK
Browse for ePub file of book in Calibre Library folder and double click on it.
Click OK when prompted and preview your book.

Go to your Calibre Library folder and find the MOBI file there created by the Kindle Previewer.
Move to your own folder for publishing to Amazon for loading when you're ready.

Publish on Amazon Notes

Book ASIN or ISBN

Title

Sub-title

Categories

Tags

Digital Rights Management

Price and Royalty

Book Blurb Notes

Upload MOBI file and Cover Image
Download Preview file to check after conversion
Check on online previewer
Select Save and Publish

Notes

Format for CreateSpace

(If using a CreateSpace Template, copy and paste manuscript as instructed)

Book Size :______________________________
Paper Colour :______________________________
ISBN :______________________________
:______________________________
:______________________________
:______________________________

Page Numbers

Insert book's front matter

Set Indents and Spacing – Settings for this book

Alignment :______________________________
Indentation :______________________________
Spacing :______________________________
Set Book Size :______________________________
Set Margins and Gutter :______________________________
:______________________________

Check that there are page breaks before each chapter and that all chapters will begin on a right hand side page in the final printing :______________________________

Fonts used for this book :______________________________

Check page numbers of each chapter and create table of contents :______________________________

Add author bio and previews of other books to back matter

Save As PDF :__________________________
Add New Title from CreateSpace dashboard :__________________________
ISBN :__________________________
:__________________________
Follow Guided Setup and load PDF & Cover :__________________________
Download proof and check online also :__________________________
Order and review proofs :__________________________
Approve for sale and distribution :__________________________
:__________________________

Cover Design Information

Vision Notes & Sketches

Cover Design

Images Used :

Image & Source :______________________________
Image & Source :______________________________
Image & Source :______________________________
:______________________________
:______________________________
:______________________________

Notes to Designer or Self

Final Cover Information:

Title Font, Size & colour :______________________________
Author Font, Size & colour :______________________________
Sub-title Information :______________________________
:______________________________
:______________________________
:______________________________

Designer Information & Contact Details :______________________________

Cost of Cover & Breakdown :______________________________

IMPORTANT INFORMATION:
(ISBN, ASIN, TAX, etc)

PROCRASTINATION PALACE

When the words don't flow, don't feel bad. It happens to all scribblers at some point or another. Sometimes it's just a little blockage that can be shifted with a bit of artful procrastination.

Try a story jigsaw. Get yourself a pad of small sticky notes, or just cut out some small squares from scrap paper you have lying around, and write bits and pieces of your current manuscript on them. Also write ideas you have for the as yet unwritten book. Then do a shuffle and lay them out in front of you, move them around. Draw a stick figure of each of your characters on them and have a couple of conversations. You might not want to do this in a coffee shop unless everyone there already knows that you're a writer and will take no notice at all.

Write out in depth character evaluations on your characters, right down to favourite colours, the schools they attended, their birthdays, and all their mental quirks. This is fabulous for breaking blocks because the characters often come up with their own ideas for what could happen next.

Doodle some bad art, scribble, colour, anything at all—just do it here, in this book, and you're unlikely to stray too far from your writing goals.

Author Brand Notes

Image Used (author image across all sites) :

Image & Source :________________________________
:________________________________
:________________________________
:________________________________
:________________________________
:________________________________

Notes on author branding. What do I want to convey and share?

Sites to use:

Blog :________________________________
Website :________________________________
Twitter :________________________________
Google+ :________________________________
Facebook :________________________________
Linkedin :________________________________
Pintrest :________________________________
Instagram :________________________________
:________________________________
:________________________________
:________________________________
:________________________________

Notes

Author Bio:

Author Press Kit:

Promotion Schedule:

Notes:

Promotion Schedule:

Notes:

Courses/Seminars/Groups:

Notes:

Notes:

Notes:

Notes:

www.ingramcontent.com/pod-product-compliance
Lightning Source LLC
Chambersburg PA
CBHW081215280526
45787CB00006B/2413
9781533636720